English Reading Comprehension
For the Spanish Speaker

Book 1

For Ages 10 - Adult

Written by
Kathleen Fisher

Illustrated by
Tracee Schmidt

Fisher Hill   Huntington Beach   California

Copyright 2006 by Kathleen Fisher
Second Printing 2008
Third Printing 2013
All rights reserved.

Published by FISHER HILL
5267 Warner Avenue, #166
Huntington Beach, CA 92649-4079

Made in the U.S.A.

Publisher's Cataloging in Publication

Fisher, Kathleen S., 1952-
     English reading comprehension for the Spanish speaker.
Book 1 / by Kathleen Fisher. --1st ed.
     p. cm.
     Audience: Ages 10-adult.
     Includes bibliographical references and index.
       ISBN 978-1-878253-37-8

     1. English language--Textbooks for foreign speakers--
Spanish. 2. English as a second language.

Table of Contents

Introduction v

Lesson 1   Animals 1

Lesson 2   People 8

Lesson 3   Places 15

Lesson 4   Things 22

Lesson 5   Action Words 29

Lesson 6   Food 36

Lesson 7   Transportation 43

Lesson 8   Colors 50

Lesson 9   Clothes 57

Lesson 10   Home 64

Lesson 11   Describing Words 71

Lesson 12   Plurals 78

Lesson 13   Words With Multiple Meanings 85

Lesson 14   Numbers 92

Lesson 15   More Things 99

Lesson 16   Nature 106

Lesson 17   More Action Words 113

Lesson 18   More Action Words 120

Lesson 19   More Animals 127

Lesson 20   Sounds 134

English Translation of Spanish Directions 141

Index 152

Contenido

Introducción.. vi

Lección 1   Los animales.. 1

Lección 2   Las personas... 8

Lección 3   Los lugares.. 15

Lección 4   Las cosas.. 22

Lección 5   Palabras de acción.. 29

Lección 6   Alimentos.. 36

Lección 7   Transporte... 43

Lección 8   Colores.. 50

Lección 9   Ropa... 57

Lección 10   Cosas que se encontrarían en una casa............................... 64

Lección 11   Palabras de descripción... 71

Lección 12   Plurales... 78

Lección 13   Palabras con múltiples significados................................... 85

Lección 14   Números... 92

Lección 15   Más cosas... 99

Lección 16   La naturaleza.. 106

Lección 17   Más palabras de acción.. 113

Lección 18   Más palabras de acción.. 120

Lección 19   Más animales... 127

Lección 20   Palabras que imitan sonidos.. 134

Traducción al inglés de las instrucciones en español............................ 141

Índice.. 152

Introduction

The purpose of this book is to help Spanish speakers improve their English reading comprehension skills. Reading comprehension is the ability to draw meaning from written words. This is an excellent book to use after finishing *English Reading and Spelling for the Spanish Speaker Book 1* because both books use the same speech sounds and high frequency words.

This book is made up of twenty lessons. Lessons include practice with fluency, vocabulary, visualization, comprehension, phonology and phonics. This book is bilingual. The directions are in Spanish. THE ENGLISH TRANSLATIONS FOR THE SPANISH DIRECTIONS ARE LOCATED AT THE BACK OF THE BOOK. There is an answer key at the end of each lesson.

Reading smoothly (fluency) is an important skill. Fluency allows readers to think about what they are reading instead of having to think about sounding out words. Decoding skills need to be learned and practiced so these skills become automatic when reading words. Visualizing (making pictures in your head) helps readers remember what they have read. Good vocabulary skills help readers visualize. Readers cannot visualize a word if they do not know its meaning. All of these skills: fluency, visualizing, vocabulary, and decoding are necessary for reading comprehension.

Reading comprehension is the goal of reading. Reading is an essential skill for jobs and daily life. Many people enjoy reading and say it is one of their favorite pastimes. Others read only when it is necessary. Whichever the case may be, everyone needs to know how to read. Learning to read comes more easily to some people than others. Most people need to be taught how to read. It is different from learning how to talk. Learning to read can be a very difficult for some people, but with practice, most everyone can learn how to read.

Introducción

Comprensión de lectura en inglés para el hispanohablante Libro 1 se escribió para ayudar a quienes hablan español a mejorar su habilidad de comprensión de la lectura en inglés. La comprensión de la lectura es la facultad de extraer significado de las palabras escritas. Este es un libro excelente para usarse después de terminar *Lectura y escritura en inglés para el hispanohablante Libro 1*, ya que ambos libros usan los mismos sonidos del habla y las mismas palabras de alta frecuencia.

Este libro está compuesto de veinte lecciones. Las lecciones incluyen la práctica de las habilidades de fluidez, vocabulario, visualización, comprensión y decodificación. Este libro es bilingüe. Las instrucciones están en español. LA TRADUCCIÓN AL INGLÉS DE LAS INSTRUCCIONES EN ESPAÑOL SE ENCUENTRA EN LAS ÚLTIMAS PÁGINAS DEL LIBRO. Hay una clave de respuestas al final de cada lección.

El leer sin interrupciones (la fluidez) es una habilidad importante. La fluidez permite a los lectores pensar lo que están leyendo en lugar de tener que pensar en pronunciar las palabras. Las habilidades de decodificación deben aprenderse y practicarse para que estas habilidades se hagan automáticas cuando se leen las palabras. La visualización (formar imágenes en su cabeza) ayuda a los lectores a recordar lo que han leído. Las habilidades del buen vocabulario ayudan a los lectores a visualizar. Los lectores no pueden visualizar una palabra si no saben lo que significa. Todas estas habilidades: la fluidez, la visualización, el vocabulario y la decodificación son necesarias para tener una buena comprensión de la lectura.

La comprensión de la lectura es la meta de la lectura. Leer es una habilidad esencial para los empleos y la vida diaria. Mucha gente disfruta de la lectura y dice que es uno de sus pasatiempos favoritos. Otros leen sólo cuando es necesario. Cualquiera que sea el caso, todos necesitan saber cómo leer. El aprender a leer es más fácil para algunas personas. La mayoría de las personas necesitan que se les enseñe cómo leer. Es diferente que aprender a hablar. Para algunas personas, aprender a leer puede ser algo muy difícil, pero con práctica, casi todos pueden aprender a leer.

Lesson 1 * Lección 1

Vocabulary * Vocabulario

Animals * Los animales

cat
gato

fish
pescado

deer
venado

clam
almeja

bee
abeja

sheep
oveja

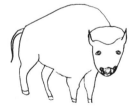

ox
buey

dog
perro

fox
zorro

rat
ratón

bug
insecto

pig
cerdo

Fill in the Blanks * Llene el Espacio

Llene cada espacio con una palabra de la página de vocabulario. Use la figura al final de la oración para ayudarse. Lea la oración con cuidado porque puede necesitar añadir una s o las letras es a la palabra del vocabulario.

1. The _____pig_____ lay in the mud.

2. We will not feed the _____deer_____ .

3. We see big _____fish_____ in the water.

4. The _____cats_____ are sleeping in the shed.

5. Do not step on the _____bug_____ .

6. The _____bee_____ sat on the cup.

7. Where are the _____sheep_____ ?

8. The _____ run to their den.

9. There are _____ in the shack.

10. You can pet the _____ .

11. We will pay cash for the three big _____ .

12. The _____ is stuck in the mud.

2

Visualizing * Visualización

Visualizar lo que lee le ayudará a recordar lo que ha leído.

Lea cada oración y después dibuje una figura de lo que ve en su mente cuando lee la oración.

The gulls sit on the dock.

In the grass, there is a red van with a green frog on top.

Fluency * Fluidez

Fluidez es la facultad de leer a un ritmo rápido sin detenerse mucho a identificar palabras. Con buena fluidez, una persona puede pensar acerca de lo que está leyendo en lugar de batallar con la pronunciación de las palabras.

Practique leyendo la historia que está a continuación hasta que tenga buena fluidez. Debe poder leer esta historia en menos de un minuto.

Pigs

A pig is an animal. Pigs live in pens. They lay in mud. On hot days the mud keeps them cool. Pigs rush to the farmer when he feeds them. They squeal and grunt to get their food. Baby pigs are piglets. It's fun to see piglets run on their short legs. Big pigs are hogs. We get ham from pigs.

Lea las palabras, primero de arriba a abajo y luego de izquierda a derecha. Practique leyendo las palabras hasta que pueda leerlas sin pausas y a un ritmo rápido.

pig	run	hot
dig	sun	pot
wig	bun	lot
big	fun	not
fig	gun	got

Comprehension * Comprensión

Llene los espacios con las palabras correctas de la historia acerca de **Pigs**.

1. A _____ is an animal.

2. Pigs live in _____ .

3. The _____ feeds the pigs.

4. Baby pigs are _____ .

5. Big pigs are _____ .

6. We get _____ from pigs.

Conteste las siguientes preguntas en oraciones completas. Cada oración debe tener un sujeto y un verbo. Comience cada oración con una mayúscula y termínela con un signo de puntuación.

7. **What is the story about?**

   _____

8. **Why do pigs lay in mud?**

   _____

9. **Who feeds the pigs?**

   _____

10. **Why do we need pigs?**

   _____

Alphabetizing * Colocar en orden alfabético

Coloque en orden alfabético las palabras correspondientes a las figuras que están a continuación. Colocar en orden alfabético significa poner las palabras según el lugar que sus letras ocupan en el alfabeto. Escriba primero las palabras que comienzan con <u>a</u>, luego las que comienzan con <u>b</u>, después <u>c</u>, <u>d</u>, <u>e</u>, y así sucesivamente. Si dos palabras comienzan con la misma letra, entonces considere la siguiente letra y escriba la palabra que tenga la segunda letra más cercana al principio del alfabeto.

a b c d e f g h l j k l m n o p q r s t u v w x y z

1. _____

2. _____

3. _____

4. _____

5. _____

6. _____

7. _____

8. _____

9. _____

10. _____

11. _____

12. _____

Answer Key * Las Respuestas

Fill in the Blanks * Llene el Espacio (page 2)

1. pigs
2. deer
3. fish
4. cats
5. bug
6. bee
7. sheep
8. foxes
9. rats
10. dog
11. clams
12. ox

Visualizing * Visualización (page 3)

Comprehension * Comprensión (page 5)

1.	pig	4.	piglets
2.	pens	5.	hogs
3.	farmer	6.	ham

7. The story is about pigs.
8. Pigs lay in mud to keep cool.
9. The farmer feeds the pigs.
10. We get ham from pigs.

Alphabetizing * Colocar en orden alfabético (page 6)

1.	bee	7.	fish
2.	bug	8.	fox
3.	cat	9.	ox
4.	clam	10.	pig
5.	deer	11.	rat
6.	dog	12.	sheep

Lesson 2 * Lección 2

Vocabulary * Vocabulario

People * Las personas

man
hombre

dad
papá

mom
mamá

kid
niño/niña

queen
reina

men
hombres

cop
policía

boss
jefe

pals/friends
amigos/amigas

lad
niño

nun
monja

vet
veterinario

Fill in the Blanks * Llene el Espacio

Llene cada espacio con una palabra de la página de vocabulario.
Use la figura al final de la oración para ayudarse. Lea la oración
con cuidado porque puede necesitar añadir una s o las letras es a la
palabra del vocabulario.

1. Ten _____ swam at the bay.

2. A _____ sits on the rock.

3. Six _____ pray with the kids.

4. Your _____ can shop at the mall.

5. Four _____ play with the dog.

6. Whose dog is with the _____ ?

7. The _____ are at the shack .

8. His _____ will meet the queen.

9. The cab will stop for the _____ .

10. We will jog with the _____ .

11. Where will the _____ sit?

12. Your _____ will stay here.

Visualizing * Visualización

Visualizar lo que lee le ayudará a recordar lo que ha leído.

Lea cada oración y después dibuje una figura de lo que ve en su mente cuando lee la oración.

Dad cuts the green grass.

The men rush to the top of the hill.

Fluency * Fluidez

Fluidez es la facultad de leer a un ritmo rápido sin detenerse mucho a identificar palabras. Con buena fluidez, una persona puede pensar acerca de lo que está leyendo en lugar de batallar con la pronunciación de las palabras.

Practique leyendo la historia que está a continuación hasta que tenga buena fluidez. Debe poder leer esta historia en menos de un minuto.

The Vet

Tom has a sick pet. He will take it to the vet. A vet is an animal doctor. The vet will help. The vet will check Tom's dog. Tom tells the vet about his dog. Tom tells the vet that his dog fell. Tom's pet gets a shot in the leg. Tom is glad that his dog will get well. Tom is glad he took his pet to the vet.

Lea las palabras, primero de arriba a abajo y luego de izquierda a derecha. Practique leyendo las palabras hasta que pueda leerlas sin pausas y a un ritmo rápido.

sick	vet	glad
pick	bet	sad
stick	pet	had
click	met	mad
chick	get	dad

Comprehension * Comprensión

Llene los espacios con las palabras correctas de la historia acerca de
The Vet.

1. A _____ is an animal doctor.

2. Tom has a _____ pet.

3. The vet will _____ Tom's pet.

4. Tom's dog _____ .

5. Tom's pet will get a _____ in the leg.

6. Vets _____ pets.

Conteste las siguientes preguntas en oraciones completas. Cada oración debe tener un sujeto y un verbo. Comience cada oración con una mayúscula y termínela con un signo de puntuación.

7. **Who is a vet?**

    _____

8. **Why did Tom take his pet to the vet?**

    _____

9. **What did the vet do?**

    _____

10. **Why is Tom glad?**

    _____

Word Families * Familias de palabras

Las palabras que riman son palabras que comienzan de manera diferente pero terminan con la misma vocal y los mismos sonidos en la terminación. Por ejemplo, *red, bed* y *said* son palabras que riman. No necesitan escribirse igual, pero necesitan terminar con la misma vocal y los mismos sonidos en la terminación.

Escriba las palabras correspondientes a las figuras bajo la rima correcta.

an	og	ug	en
1.	5.	9.	13.
2.	6.	10.	14.
3.	7.	11.	15.
4.	8.	12.	16.

Answer Key * Las Respuestas

Fill in the Blanks * Llene el Espacio (page 9)

1. men
2. lad
3. nuns
4. pals/friends
5. kids
6. vet
7. cops
8. dad
9. man
10. boss
11. queen
12. mom

Visualizing * Visualización (page 10)

Comprehension * Comprensión (page 12)

1.	vet	4.	fell
2.	sick	5.	shot
3.	check	6.	help

7. A vet is an animal doctor.
8. Tom's pet was sick.
9. The vet gave Tom's dog a shot.
10. Tom is glad that his dog will get well and that he took him to the vet.

Word Families * Familias de palabras (page 13)

an	og	ug	en
1. fan	5. dog	9. bug	13. men
2. van	6. log	10. hug	14. hen
3. man	7. frog	11. rug	15. ten
4. pan	8. hog	12. mug	16. pen

Lesson 3 * Lección 3

Vocabulary * Vocabulario

Places * Los lugares

bay
bahía

club
club

creek
arroyo

hill
colina

shed
cobertizo

shack
cabaña

shop
talleer

dock
muelle

mill
molino

reef
arrecife

den
guarida

bog
pantano

Fill in the Blanks * Llene el Espacio

Llene cada espacio con una palabra de la página de vocabulario. Use la figura al final de la oración para ayudarse. Lea la oración con cuidado porque puede necesitar añadir una <u>s</u> o las letras <u>es</u> a la palabra del vocabulario.

1. I can hear ducks at the _____ .

2. The raft got stuck in the _____ .

3. The fox sleeps in its _____ .

4. Let's toss rocks into the _____ .

5. There is no water at the _____ .

6. Do not cut your leg at the _____ .

7. The kids play at the _____ .

8. The dogs sleep in the _____ .

9. The men have fun at the _____ .

10. Let's swim to the _____ .

11. There are three trees on top of the _____ .

12. Let's meet at the _____ .

Visualizing * Visualización

Visualizar lo que lee le ayudará a recordar lo que ha leído.

Lea cada oración y después dibuje una figura de lo que ve en su mente cuando lee la oración.

The big kids with red hats will fish from the dock.

In the shed, the ducks and sheep sleep on the hay.

Fluency * Fluidez

Fluidez es la facultad de leer a un ritmo rápido sin detenerse mucho a identificar palabras. Con buena fluidez, una persona puede pensar acerca de lo que está leyendo en lugar de batallar con la pronunciación de las palabras.

Practique leyendo la historia que está a continuación hasta que tenga buena fluidez. Debe poder leer esta historia en menos de un minuto.

The Reef

A reef is a fun place. A reef is a strip of rock, sand, or coral. You can swim at the reef. The sun feels good at the reef. You can see fish at a reef. You can swim with big and small fish. Fish live at the reef. But you must be careful because the reef is sharp. You can cut your leg on the reef.

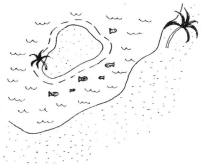

Lea las palabras, primero de arriba a abajo y luego de izquierda a derecha. Practique leyendo las palabras hasta que pueda leerlas sin pausas y a un ritmo rápido.

beep	fish	leg
jeep	dish	beg
steep	swish	Meg
creep	wish	egg
deep	shush	peg

Comprehension * Comprensión

Llene los espacios con las palabras correctas de la historia acerca de **The Reef**.

1. **A reef is a** _____ **place.**

2. **We can** _____ **at the reef.**

3. **The sun** _____ **good at the reef.**

4. **We can see** _____ **at the reef.**

5. **Fish** _____ **at the reef.**

6. **You can** _____ **your leg on the reef.**

Conteste las siguientes preguntas en oraciones completas. Cada oración debe tener un sujeto y un verbo. Comience cada oración con una mayúscula y termínela con un signo de puntuación.

7. **What is a reef?**

   _____

8. **What can you do at the reef?**

   _____

9. **Who lives at the reef?**

   _____

10. **Why must you be careful at the reef?**

    _____

Vowel Sounds * Sonidos de las vocales

Llene los espacios con las vocales correspondientes. Las vocales son <u>a</u>, <u>e</u>, <u>i</u>, <u>o</u>, <u>u</u> y a veces <u>y</u>. Cada palabra o sílaba necesita un sonido vocal.

1. Th__ d__cks sw__m __n th__ b__y.

2. D__ n__t c__t y__ __r l__g __n th__ r__ __f.

3. Th__ k__ds r__n __p th__ h__ll.

4. __ne m__n w__ll f__sh fr__m th__ d__ck.

5. Th__ sh__p h__s d__shes, c__ps, __nd gl__sses.

6. Th__ boat __s st__ck __n th__ b__g.

7. Thr__ __ m__n pl__y dr__ms __t th__ cl__b.

8. Th__r__ __re b__g f__sh __n th__ cr__ __k.

9. Th__ f__x sl__ __ps __n h__s d__n.

10. L__ck th__ sh__d.

11. Th__r__ __s water __t th__ m__ll.

12. Wh__r__ __s th__ sh__ck?

20

Answer Key * Las Respuestas

Fill in the Blanks * Llene el Espacio (page 16)

1. bay
2. bog
3. den
4. creek
5. mill
6. reef
7. shack
8. shed
9. club
10. dock
11. hill
12. shop

Visualizing * Visualización (page 17)

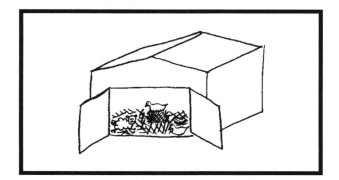

Comprehension * Comprensión (page 19)

1.	fun	4.	fish
2.	swim	5.	live
3.	feels	6.	cut

7. A reef is a strip of rock, sand, or coral.
8. You can swim at the reef.
9. Fish live at the reef.
10. You must be careful because the reef is sharp.

Vowel Sounds * Sonidos de las vocales (page 20)

1. The ducks swim in the bay.
2. Do not cut your leg on the reef.
3. The kids run up the hill.
4. One man will fish from the dock.
5. The shop has dishes, cups, and glasses.
6. The boat is stuck in the bog.
7. Three men play drums at the club.
8. There are big fish in the creek.
9. The fox sleeps in his den.
10. Lock the shed.
11. There is water at the mill.
12. Where is the shack?

Lesson 4 * Lección 4

Vocabulary * Vocabulario

Things * Las cosas

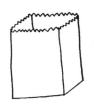

bag
bolsa

rag
paño

bell
campana

log
tronco

rod
caña

box
caja

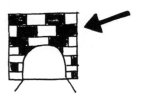

brick
ladrillo

drum
tambor

doll
muñeca

lock
candado

rock
roca

sack
saco

Fill in the Blanks * Llene el Espacio

Llene cada espacio con una palabra de la página de vocabulario. Use la figura al final de la oración para ayudarse. Lea la oración con cuidado porque puede necesitar añadir una s o las letras es a la palabra del vocabulario.

1. **You can fish with the red** _____ .

2. **Your** _____ **is on the bed.**

3. **Do not tap on the** _____ .

4. **Let's sit on the** _____ .

5. **I hear a** _____ **and a drum.**

6. **The pups can sleep in the** _____ .

7. **The** _____ **are in the shed.**

8. **We have red and green** _____ .

9. **Do not** _____ **the box.**

10. **The pan is in the big** _____ .

11. **A frog is on the** _____ .

12. **Fill the** _____ **with clams.**

Visualizing * Visualización

Visualizar lo que lee le ayudará a recordar lo que ha leído.

Lea cada oración y después dibuje una figura de lo que ve en su mente cuando lee la oración.

Under the tree, the doll sits on the bricks.

At the club, the man plays the drums.

Fluency * Fluidez

Fluidez es la facultad de leer a un ritmo rápido sin detenerse mucho a identificar palabras. Con buena fluidez, una persona puede pensar acerca de lo que está leyendo en lugar de batallar con la pronunciación de las palabras.

Practique leyendo la historia que está a continuación hasta que tenga buena fluidez. Debe poder leer esta historia en menos de un minuto.

Drums

Drums are fun to play. You can play drums at a club. You can play drums in a shed. Kids like to play drums. They like to tap, tap, tap on the drum. People like to hip-hop to the beat of a drum. Drummers can tap fast or slow on the drum with their drumsticks. Some drummers toss their sticks in the air.

Lea las palabras, primero de arriba a abajo y luego de izquierda a derecha. Practique leyendo las palabras hasta que pueda leerlas sin pausas y a un ritmo rápido.

drum	play	toss
hum	day	boss
bum	may	moss
strum	pray	gloss
sum	sway	loss

Comprehension * Comprensión

Llene los espacios con las palabras correctas de la historia acerca de
Drums.

1. _____ are fun to play.

2. **You can** _____ **drums at a club.**

3. **Kids like to** _____ **on a drum.**

4. **People like to** _____ **to the beat of a drum.**

5. **Drummers can tap fast with their** _____ .

6. **Some drummers** _____ **their sticks in the air.**

Conteste las siguientes preguntas en oraciones completas. Cada
oración debe tener un sujeto y un verbo. Comience cada oración
con una mayúscula y termínela con un signo de puntuación.

7. **Where can you play a drum?**

   _____

8. **Who likes to play drums?**

   _____

9. **What do you do with drumsticks?**

   _____

10. **Would you like to play the drums? Why?**

    _____

Categories * Categorías

Escriba el nombre de cada figura en la categoría correcta.

Animals	People	Places	Things

Answer Key * Las Respuestas

Fill in the Blanks * Llene el Espacio (page 23)

1. rod
2. doll
3. drum
4. log
5. bell
6. box

7. bricks
8. rags
9. lock
10. bag
11. rock
12. sack

Visualizing * Visualización (page 24)

Comprehension * Comprensión (page 26)

1. Drums	4. hip-hop
2. play	5. drumsticks
3. tap	6. toss

7. You can a drum at a club or in a shed.
8. Kids like to play drums.
9. You can tap fast or slow on the drums with your drumsticks.
10. *Answers will vary.*

Categories * Categorías (page 27)

Animals	People	Places	Things
fish	queen	creek	bag
bee	man	shed	bell
dog	dad	hill	log
fox	kid	bay	lock

Lesson 5 * Lección 5

Vocabulary * Vocabulario

Action Words * Palabras de acción

Coloque las palabras de vocabulario en inglés en orden alfabético. Para hacerlo, escriba primero las palabras que comienzan con <u>a</u>, luego las que comienzan con <u>b</u>, después <u>c</u>, <u>d</u>, <u>e</u>, y así sucesivamente. Si dos palabras comienzan con la misma letra, entonces considere la siguiente letra y escriba la palabra que tenga la segunda letra más cercana al principio del alfabeto.

English	Spanish	Alphabetize
1. fill	morder	1.
2. buzz	zumbido	2.
3. flee	aplaudir	3.
4. grab	cortar	4.
5. dig	cavar	5.
6. hear	dejar caer	6.
7. fell	caer	7.
8. fix	arreglar	8.
9. clap	escapar	9.
10. get	conseguir	10.
11. cut	sujetar	11.
12. drop	escuchar	12.
13. bit	llenar	13.
14. feed	alimentar	14.

Fill in the Blanks * Llene el Espacio

Llene cada espacio con una palabra de la página de vocabulario. Use la figura al final de la oración para ayudarse. Lea la oración con cuidado porque puede necesitar añadir una <u>s</u> o las letras <u>es</u> a la palabra del vocabulario.

1. The dog _____ the man's leg.

2. Bees _____ in the tree.

3. The robbers _____ from the bank.

4. She _____ the dog at six o'clock.

5. Six kids _____ a big hole.

6. Mom _____ her glass with water.

7. Dad _____ ham and eggs for the kids.

8. Do not _____ my leg!

9. She _____ the kids playing in the shed.

10. He _____ a fax from his mom.

11. The fox _____ off the big rock.

12. He _____ his leg in the crash.

13. Do not _____ until they finish.

14. Meg slips and _____ her snack.

Visualizing * Visualización

Visualizar lo que lee le ayudará a recordar lo que ha leído.

Lea cada oración y después dibuje una figura de lo que ve en su mente cuando lee la oración.

The man fell off the ship.

Pam drops the frog into the water.

Fluency * Fluidez

Fluidez es la facultad de leer a un ritmo rápido sin detenerse mucho a identificar palabras. Con buena fluidez, una persona puede pensar acerca de lo que está leyendo en lugar de batallar con la pronunciación de las palabras.

Practique leyendo la historia que está a continuación hasta que tenga buena fluidez. Debe poder leer esta historia en menos de un minuto.

Play

Kids like to play. They like to run. Some kids run fast. Some kids run slow. Kids like to hop. Kids like to skip. At the beach, kids run and jump in the water. They swim in the water. Sometimes dogs swim in the water. On the sand, kids like to dig and make sand castles. They fill buckets with water. Some kids toss a Frisbee at the beach. At home, kids sometimes sit and play a quiet game.

Lea las palabras, primero de arriba a abajo y luego de izquierda a derecha. Practique leyendo las palabras hasta que pueda leerlas sin pausas y a un ritmo rápido.

cap	an	cat
map	fan	sat
sap	man	bat
slap	bran	brat
trap	can	flat

Comprehension * Comprensión

Llene los espacios con las palabras correctas de la historia acerca de **Play**.

1. Kids like to _____ .

2. At the beach, kids swim in the _____ .

3. Sometimes dogs _____ in the water.

4. Kids like to _____ in the sand.

5. They _____ buckets with water.

6. Some kids _____ a Frisbee.

7. At home, kids may play a _____ game.

Conteste las siguientes preguntas en oraciones completas. Cada oración debe tener un sujeto y un verbo. Comience cada oración con una mayúscula y termínela con un signo de puntuación.

8. What do you like to play?

_____

9. Do you go to the beach?

_____

10. Do you know how to toss a Frisbee?

_____

Rhyming Words * Palabras que riman

Las palabras que riman son palabras que comienzan de manera diferente pero terminan con la misma vocal y los mismos sonidos en la terminación. Por ejemplo, *red, bed* y *said* son palabras que riman. No necesitan escribirse igual, pero necesitan terminar con la misma vocal y los mismos sonidos en la terminación.

Escriba dos palabras que rimen con cada una de las palabras del vocabulario.

Vocabulary Word	Rhyming Word	Rhyming Word
1. bit		
2. buzz		
3. cut		
4. dig		
5. drop		
6. fell		
7. fix		
8. flee		
9. get		
10. grab		
11. hear		
12. fill		
13. feed		
14. clap		

Answer Key * Las Respuestas

Alphabetizing * Colocar en orden alfabético (page 29)

1.	bit	5.	dig	9.	fill	13.grab	
2.	buzz	6.	drop	10.	fix	14.hear	
3.	clap	7.	feed	11.	flee		
4.	cut	8.	fell	12.	get		

Fill in the Blanks * Llene el Espacio (page 30)

1. bit
2. buzz
3. flee
4. feeds
5. dig
6. fills
7. fixes
8. grab
9. hears
10. gets
11. fell
12. cut
13. clap
14. drops

Visualizing * Visualización (page 31)

Comprehension * Comprensión (page 33)

1.	play	5.	fill
2.	water	6.	toss
3.	swim	7.	quiet
4.	dig		

8. *Answers will vary.*
9. *Answers will vary.*
10. *Answers will vary.*

Rhyming Words * Palabras que riman (page 34)
1–14. *Answers will vary. The following are examples.*

	Vocabulary Word	Rhyming Word	Rhyming Word
1.	bit	sit	lit
2.	buzz	fuzz	was
3.	cut	mutt	but
4.	dig	big	twig
5.	drop	mop	cop
6.	fell	bell	well
7.	fix	mix	picks
8.	flee	bee	me
9.	get	wet	pet
10.	grab	cab	tab
11.	hear	deer	fear
12.	fill	bill	pill
13.	feed	need	seed
14.	clap	slap	cap

Lesson 6 * Lección 6

Vocabulary * Vocabulario

Food * Alimentos

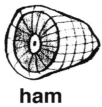

ham
jamón

jam
mermelada

beef
carne de res

clam
almeja

eggs
huevos

gum
chicle

fish
pescado

fig
higo

beets
remolachas

water
agua

hot dogs
"perros calientes"

yams
camotes

36

Fill in the Blanks * Llene el Espacio

Llene cada espacio con una palabra de la página de vocabulario. Use la figura al final de la oración para ayudarse. Lea la oración con cuidado porque puede necesitar añadir una <u>s</u> o las letras <u>es</u> a la palabra del vocabulario.

1. We had _____ at the picnic.

2. The _____ are sweet.

3. Fresh _____ are on the red mat.

4. Here is the _____ .

5. I can smell the _____ .

6. Put the ten _____ in a bag.

7. The hen lays six _____ .

8. She puts _____ on her bread.

9. _____ is good for you.

10. Put the _____ on the green dish.

11. She chews _____ all day long.

12. Dad likes _____ and eggs.

Visualizing * Visualización

Visualizar lo que lee le ayudará a recordar lo que ha leído.

Lea cada oración y después dibuje una figura de lo que ve en su mente cuando lee la oración.

Ted puts four hot dogs on the dish.

Pam picked ten figs off the tree.

Fluency * Fluidez

Fluidez es la facultad de leer a un ritmo rápido sin detenerse mucho a identificar palabras. Con buena fluidez, una persona puede pensar acerca de lo que está leyendo en lugar de batallar con la pronunciación de las palabras.

Practique leyendo la historia que está a continuación hasta que tenga buena fluidez. Debe poder leer esta historia en menos de un minuto.

Food

   We like to eat food. Kids like to eat hot dogs and drink pop. We get food from plants and animals. Beef comes from cows. Ham comes from pigs. Eggs come from hens. Figs come from trees. A yam is the root of a plant. Some people drink six cups of water a day. Some people do not like the smell of fish. We eat food with our families and friends.

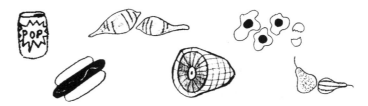

Lea las palabras, primero de arriba a abajo y luego de izquierda a derecha. Practique leyendo las palabras hasta que pueda leerlas sin pausas y a un ritmo rápido.

ham	day	dog
jam	play	frog
gram	sway	log
swam	gray	hog
slam	stay	smog

Comprehension * Comprensión

Llene los espacios con las palabras correctas de la historia acerca de **Food**.

1. **We like to eat** _____ .

2. _____ **comes from cows.**

3. **Hens lay** _____ .

4. **Figs come from** _____ .

5. **A yam is the** _____ **of a plant.**

6. **We eat food with our families and** _____ .

Conteste las siguientes preguntas en oraciones completas. Cada oración debe tener un sujeto y un verbo. Comience cada oración con una mayúscula y termínela con un signo de puntuación.

7. **What do you like to eat?**

   _____

8. **What do you like to drink?**

   _____

9. **How many cups of water do you drink a day?**

   _____

10. **Do you like the smell of fish?**

   _____

Alphabetizing * Colocar en orden alfabético

Coloque en orden alfabético las palabras correspondientes a las figuras que están a continuación. Colocar en orden alfabético significa poner las palabras según el lugar que sus letras ocupan en el alfabeto. Las palabras que comienzan con <u>a</u> van primero (si existen), luego la palabras que comienzan con <u>b</u>, seguidas de las que comienzan con <u>c</u>, luego <u>d</u>, luego <u>e</u>, hasta que todas la palabras se hayan colocado en orden alfabético. Si dos palabras comienzan con la misma letra, entonces considere la siguiente letra y escriba la palabra que tenga la segunda letra más cercana al principio del alfabeto.

a b c d e f g h l j k l m n o p q r s t u v w x y z

1. _____

2. _____

3. _____

4. _____

5. _____

6. _____

7. _____

8. _____

9. _____

10. _____

11. _____

12. _____

Answer Key * Las Respuestas

Fill in the Blanks * Llene el Espacio (page 37)

1. hot dogs
2. yams
3. clams
4. beef
5. fish
6. figs
7. eggs
8. jam
9. Water
10. beets
11. gum
12. ham

Visualizing * Visualización (page 38)

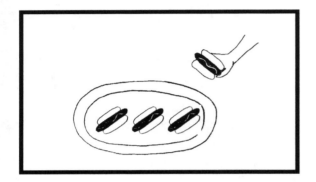
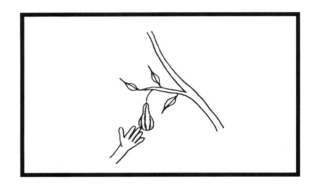

Comprehension * Comprensión (page 40)

1.	food	4.	trees
2.	Beef	5.	root
3.	eggs	6.	friends

7. *Answers will vary.*
8. *Answers will vary.*
9. *Answers will vary.*
10. *Answers will vary.*

Alphabetizing * Colocar en orden alfabético (page 41)

1.	beef	7.	gum
2.	beets	8.	ham
3.	clam	9.	hot dogs
4.	eggs	10.	jam
5.	fig	11.	water
6.	fish	12.	yams

Lesson 7 * Lección 7

Vocabulary * Vocabulario

Transportation * Transporte

van
camioneta

bus
autobús

jet
avión a reacción

ship
barco

sled
trineo

truck
camión

cab
taxi

sub
submarino

jeep
jeep

hot rod
auto alterado

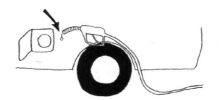

gas
gasolina

map
mapa

Fill in the Blanks * Llene el Espacio

Llene cada espacio con una palabra de la página de vocabulario. Use la figura al final de la oración para ayudarse. Lea la oración con cuidado porque puede necesitar añadir una s o las letras es a la palabra del vocabulario.

1. That _____ is quick.

2. The _____ is on the hill.

3. The _____ are stuck in the mud.

4. We can not see the _____ .

5. Four men sit in the green _____ .

6. _____ tell us where to go.

7. Mom will fill the van with _____ .

8. The _____ is at the dock.

9. The _____ crashed into the tree.

10. Ten kids are on the red _____ .

11. Our friends are on that _____ .

12. Pack the mats in the black _____ .

Visualizing * Visualización

Visualizar lo que lee le ayudará a recordar lo que ha leído.

Lea cada oración y después dibuje una figura de lo que ve en su mente cuando lee la oración.

The black truck crashed into the green van.

Ted slid down the hill on his red sled.

Fluency * Fluidez

Fluidez es la facultad de leer a un ritmo rápido sin detenerse mucho a identificar palabras. Con buena fluidez, una persona puede pensar acerca de lo que está leyendo en lugar de batallar con la pronunciación de las palabras.

Practique leyendo la historia que está a continuación hasta que tenga buena fluidez. Debe poder leer esta historia en menos de un minuto.

A Sub

A sub is a ship. A sub goes under water. A sub has a shell. Water fills the shell. The sub goes down. Air fills the shell. Men and women work on a sub. They sleep in the sub. They eat in the sub. The water is let out. The sub goes up. Then they can see the sun. Kids like to play with a toy sub in the tub.

Lea las palabras, primero de arriba a abajo y luego de izquierda a derecha. Practique leyendo las palabras hasta que pueda leerlas sin pausas y a un ritmo rápido.

ship	sub	fill
hip	tub	ill
clip	cub	spill
trip	club	drill
slip	stub	quill

Comprehension * Comprensión

Llene los espacios con las palabras correctas de la historia acerca de
A Sub.

1. A _____ is a ship.

2. A sub goes under _____ .

3. _____ and women work on a sub.

4. Air _____ the shell.

5. The water is _____ out.

6. Kids like to _____ with a sub in the tub.

Conteste las siguientes preguntas en oraciones completas. Cada oración debe tener un sujeto y un verbo. Comience cada oración con una mayúscula y termínela con un signo de puntuación.

7. **What happens when water fills the shell of a sub?**

   _____

8. **What happens when the water is let out of a sub?**

   _____

9. **Would you like to work in a sub?**

   _____

10. **Have you been on a ship?**

   _____

Vowel Sounds * Sonidos de las vocales

Llene los espacios con las vocales correspondientes. Las vocales son <u>a</u>, <u>e</u>, <u>i</u>, <u>o</u>, <u>u</u> y a veces <u>y</u>. Cada palabra o sílaba necesita un sonido vocal.

1. Wh__r__ __s th__ b__s?

2. L__t's g__t th__ r__d sl__d.

3. Th__ gr__ __n sh__p __s __t th__ d__ck.

4. T__n m__n __r__ __n th__ s__b.

5. Th__ j__ __p f__ll __n th__ cr__ __k.

6. D__d g__ts g__s f__r th__ tr__ck.

7. Th__ m__p __s __n th__ v__n.

8. My friend h__s __ fast h__t r__d.

9. P__t th__ d__gs __n th__ tr__ck.

10. D__ n__t cr__sh th__ v__n!

11. Gr__b __ c__b __nd go.

12. Th__ r__ch m__n p__ys c__sh f__r th__ gr__y j__t.

Answer Key * Las Respuestas

Fill in the Blanks * Llene el Espacio (page 44)

1. hot rod
2. sled
3. trucks
4. sub
5. jeep
6. Maps

7. gas
8. ship
9. cab
10. bus
11. jet
12. van

Visualizing * Visualización (page 45)

Comprehension * Comprensión (page 47)

1.	sub	4.	fills
2.	water	5.	let
3.	Men	6.	play

7. When water fills the shell, the sub goes down.
8. When the water is let out, the sub goes up.
9. *Answers will vary.*
10. *Answers will vary.*

Vowel Sounds * Sonidos de las vocales (page 48)

1. Where is the bus?
2. Let's get the red sled.
3. The green ship is at the dock.
4. Ten men are on the sub.
5. The jeep fell in the creek.
6. Dad gets gas for the truck.
7. The map is in the van.
8. My friend has a fast hot rod.
9. Put the dogs in the truck.
10. Do not crash the van!
11. Grab a cab and go.
12. The rich man pays cash for the gray jet.

Lesson 8 * Lección 8

Vocabulary * Vocabulario

Colors * Colores

Coloque las palabras de vocabulario en inglés en orden alfabético. Para hacerlo, escriba primero las palabras que comienzan con a, luego las que comienzan con b, después c, d, e, y así sucesivamente. Si dos palabras comienzan con la misma letra, entonces considere la siguiente letra y escriba la palabra que tenga la segunda letra más cercana al principio del alfabeto. Las últimas tres palabras de la lista son palabras visuales de alta frecuencia.

English	Spanish	Alphabetize
1. black	negro	1.
2. gray	gris	2.
3. green	verde	3.
4. red	rojo	4.
5. yellow	amarillo	5.
6. orange	naranja	6.
7. blue	azul	7.
8. white	blanco	8.
9. purple	morado	9.
10. brown	marrón	10.
11. pink	rosado	11.
12. they	ellos, ellas	12.
13. have	tener	13.
14. are	son, estar	14.

Rhyming Words * Palabras que riman

Escriba una palabra del vocabulario que rime con cada una de las palabras de la lista a continuación. Las palabras que riman son palabras que comienzan de manera diferente pero terminan con la misma vocal y los mismos sonidos en la terminación. Por ejemplo, *red, bed* y *said* son palabras que riman. No necesitan escribirse igual, pero necesitan terminar con la misma vocal y los mismos sonidos en la terminación. **Coloree** cada círculo con el color correcto.

Vocabulary Word	Rhyming Word
1.	clown
2.	mean
3.	fellow
4.	day
5.	sink
6.	said
7.	bite
8.	stack
9.	glue
10.	far
11.	pay

black

gray

green

yellow

brown

orange

blue

white

purple

pink

red

Visualizing * Visualización

Visualizar lo que lee le ayudará a recordar lo que ha leído.

Lea cada oración y después dibuje una figura de lo que ve en su mente cuando lee la oración.

The man with the yellow hat digs a deep pit.

The six kids sit in the big orange bus.

Fluency * Fluidez

Fluidez es la facultad de leer a un ritmo rápido sin detenerse mucho a identificar palabras. Con buena fluidez, una persona puede pensar acerca de lo que está leyendo en lugar de batallar con la pronunciación de las palabras.

Practique leyendo la historia que está a continuación hasta que tenga buena fluidez. Debe poder leer esta historia en menos de un minuto.

Colors

Colors are everywhere. Apples are red. The sky is blue. The sun is yellow. Cars and trucks can be many colors. You can make all colors from red, yellow, and blue. Red and yellow make orange. Carrots are orange. Yellow and blue make green. Grass is green. Blue and red make purple. Many flowers are purple. After it rains, you can sometimes see a rainbow. A rainbow has many colors.

Lea las palabras, primero de arriba a abajo y luego de izquierda a derecha. Practique leyendo las palabras hasta que pueda leerlas sin pausas y a un ritmo rápido.

red	duck	can
bed	truck	fan
fed	stuck	man
led	luck	plan
sled	pluck	bran

Comprehension * Comprensión

Llene los espacios con las palabras correctas de la historia acerca de **Colors**.

1. Colors are _____ .

2. The sun is _____ .

3. Trucks can be _____ colors.

4. You can make all the colors from blue, yellow, and _____ .

5. Blue and yellow make _____ .

6. Red and blue make _____ .

7. A _____ has many colors.

Conteste las siguientes preguntas en oraciones completas. Cada oración debe tener un sujeto y un verbo. Comience cada oración con una mayúscula y termínela con un signo de puntuación.

8. What is your favorite color?

_____

9. What are three colors in the rainbow?

_____

10. What color is your car?

_____

Sentence Anagrams * Anagramas de oraciones

Reacomode las palabras para formar oraciones completas que suenen bien. Comience encontrando la palabra de acción principal (verbo) y luego juntando las palabras para formar frases.

1. in red runs a grass fox green the

   _____

2. white is where and dog the black

   _____

3. will and figs snack they ham a have for

   _____

4. box is here blue a big

   _____

5. the do cat grab not yellow

   _____

6. deep van the is gray mud in a stuck

   _____

7. brown shed sleep the and ducks the in white

   _____

Answer Key * Las Respuestas

Alphabetizing * Colocar en orden alfabético (page 50)

1. are	5. gray	9. pink	13. white
2. black	6. green	10. purple	14. yellow
3. blue	7. have	11. red	
4. brown	8. orange	12. they	

Rhyming Words * Palabras que riman (page 51)

1. brown		7. white	
2. green		8. black	
3. yellow		9. blue	
4. gray		10. are	
5. pink		11. they	
6. red			

Visualizing * Visualización (page 52)

Comprehension * Comprensión (page 54)

1. everywhere	5. green
2. yellow	6. purple
3. many	7. rainbow
4. red	

8. *Answers will vary.*
9. *Answers will vary.*
10. *Answers will vary.*

Sentence Anagrams * Anagramas de oraciones (page 55)

1. A red fox runs in the green grass.
2. Where is the black and white dog?
3. They will have ham and figs for a snack.
4. Here is a big blue box.
5. Do not grab the yellow cat.
6. The gray van is stuck in the deep mud.
7. The brown and white ducks sleep in the shed.

Lesson 9 * Lección 9

Vocabulary * Vocabulario

Clothes * Ropa

hat
sombrero

cap
gorra

wig
peluca

sock
calcetín

dress
vestido

cuff
puño

jacket
chaqueta

glasses
anteojos

muff
manguito

smock
blusón

heel
tacón

press
planchar

57

Fill in the Blanks * Llene el Espacio

Llene cada espacio con una palabra de la página de vocabulario. Use la figura al final de la oración para ayudarse. Lea la oración con cuidado porque puede necesitar añadir una <u>s</u> o las letras <u>es</u> a la palabra del vocabulario.

1. Your shoes need new _____ .

2. The _____ has big blue pockets.

3. I need _____ to see.

4. His _____ is yellow and orange.

5. The _____ will keep your ears warm.

6. I do not want pants with _____ .

7. Will you _____ my dress?

8. Your _____ are under the bed.

9. Your friend's _____ is in the shed.

10. His mom has on a brown _____ .

11. Where are the pink and white _____ ?

12. The cat is sleeping on your _____ .

Visualizing * Visualización

Visualizar lo que lee le ayudará a recordar lo que ha leído.

Lea cada oración y después dibuje una figura de lo que ve en su mente cuando lee la oración.

She puts a pink dress on her doll.

Your blue jacket is on the bed.

Fluency * Fluidez

Fluidez es la facultad de leer a un ritmo rápido sin detenerse mucho a identificar palabras. Con buena fluidez, una persona puede pensar acerca de lo que está leyendo en lugar de batallar con la pronunciación de las palabras.

Practique leyendo la historia que está a continuación hasta que tenga buena fluidez. Debe poder leer esta historia en menos de un minuto.

Caps

People wear caps on their heads. Caps can be many colors and sizes but only one shape. Caps have a bill. This bill keeps the sun out of your eyes. Baseball players wear caps. Each baseball team has their logo on their cap. Some caps are only one color. Other caps have two or more colors. Do you have a cap? What color is your cap?

Lea las palabras, primero de arriba a abajo y luego de izquierda a derecha. Practique leyendo las palabras hasta que pueda leerlas sin pausas y a un ritmo rápido.

cap	bell	cash
slap	fell	smash
clap	smell	stash
map	shell	hash
snap	sell	dash

Comprehension * Comprensión

Llene los espacios con las palabras correctas de la historia acerca de **Caps**.

1. **You wear a cap on your** _____ .

2. **A cap has a** _____ .

3. _____ **players wear caps.**

4. **Caps keep the** _____ **out of your eyes.**

5. **Baseball teams have their** _____ **on their cap.**

6. **Some caps are only** _____ **color.**

Conteste las siguientes preguntas en oraciones completas. Cada oración debe tener un sujeto y un verbo. Comience cada oración con una mayúscula y termínela con un signo de puntuación.

7. **Do you have a cap?**

_____

8. **What color is your cap?**

_____

9. **What else can you wear on your head?**

_____

10. **Why do people wear caps?**

_____

What's Missing? * ¿Qué falta?

Complete cada oración. Falta el verbo o el sujeto de cada una de las oraciones. Después de cada oración escriba una **S** si faltaba el sujeto o una **V** si faltaba el verbo.

Ejemplo: _____ run in the park.
<u>The kids</u> run in the park.   <u>S</u>

1. The big dog _____ on the bed.   _____

2. _____ feeds the ducks in the shed.   _____

3. Dan _____ a deep pit.   _____

4. Pam _____ the bell.   _____

5. I _____ the drum.   _____

6. Sam _____ the cup with water.   _____

7. The _____ bit Tom's leg.   _____

8. _____ swims in the ocean.   _____

9. _____ fell down the steps.   _____

10. Tom _____ the van.   _____

11. Mom _____ the yellow cat.   _____

12. The _____ slid on the ice.   _____

Answer Key * Las Respuestas

Fill in the Blanks * Llene el Espacio (page 58)

1. heels
2. smock
3. glasses
4. cap
5. muffs
6. cuffs
7. press
8. socks
9. jacket
10. wig
11. dresses
12. hat

Visualizing * Visualización (page 59)

 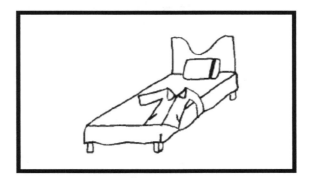

Comprehension * Comprensión (page 61)

1.	head	4.	sun
2.	bill	5.	logo
3.	Baseball	6.	one

7. *Answers will vary.*
8. *Answers will vary.*
9. *Answers will vary.*
10. *Answers will vary.*

What's Missing * ¿Qué falta? (page 62)
Answers will vary except for S (subject) or V (verb). The following are examples for the Subject or Verb parts.

1. sleeps,   V
2. Ed,   S
3. digs,   V
4. rang,   V
5. hear,   V
6. fills,   V
7. dog,   S
8. Sally,   S
9. Dad,   S
10. drives,   V
11. fed,   V
12. duck,   S

Lesson 10 * Lección 10

Vocabulary * Vocabulario

Things You'd Find At Home * Cosas que se encontrarían en una casa

rug
tapete

pan
cacerola

fan
ventilator

mop
trapeador

bed
cama

dish
plato

sheet
sábana

clock
reloj

flag
bandera

glass
vaso

brush
cepillo

trash
basura

Fill in the Blanks * Llene el Espacio

Llene cada espacio con una palabra de la página de vocabulario. Use la figura al final de la oración para ayudarse. Lea la oración con cuidado porque puede necesitar añadir una s o las letras es a la palabra del vocabulario.

1. Put the red _____ on the bed.

2. We have six green _____ .

3. She will put up the red and green _____ .

4. She _____ the floor at ten o'clock.

5. The three blue _____ are on the yellow mat.

6. Pick up your _____ and put it in the bag.

7. The kids play on the _____ .

8. He _____ his teeth after lunch.

9. Dad will fry the eggs in the _____ .

10. Your cap is on your _____ .

11. The _____ will keep us cool.

12. The _____ fell off the wall.

Visualizing * Visualización

Visualizar lo que lee le ayudará a recordar lo que ha leído.

Lea cada oración y después dibuje una figura de lo que ve en su mente cuando lee la oración.

Mom fills the six green spotted glasses with water.

The clock says six o'clock.

Fluency * Fluidez

Fluidez es la facultad de leer a un ritmo rápido sin detenerse mucho a identificar palabras. Con buena fluidez, una persona puede pensar acerca de lo que está leyendo en lugar de batallar con la pronunciación de las palabras.

Practique leyendo la historia que está a continuación hasta que tenga buena fluidez. Debe poder leer esta historia en menos de un minuto.

Beds

We sleep in beds. Some beds are hard. Some beds are soft. We sleep in bedrooms. Some bedrooms have one bed. Some bedrooms have two beds. Some kids like to sleep in bunk beds. When it's hot people sleep with just a sheet. When it is cold people sleep with a blanket or quilt. Moms tell their kids not to jump on the beds. Sometimes moms find their kids under the bed. Moms tell their kids that beds are for sleeping and not for playing.

Lea las palabras, primero de arriba a abajo y luego de izquierda a derecha. Practique leyendo las palabras hasta que pueda leerlas sin pausas y a un ritmo rápido.

kid	bunk	jump
slid	clunk	bump
grid	sunk	slump
did	junk	stump
hid	trunk	pump

Comprehension * Comprensión

Llene los espacios con las palabras correctas de la historia acerca de
Beds.

1. **We sleep** _____ **bedrooms.**

2. **Some kids like to sleep in** _____ **beds.**

3. **When it's hot people sleep with just a** _____ .

4. **Moms say, "Do not** _____ **on the bed!"**

5. **Some kids hide** _____ **the bed.**

6. **Beds are for** _____ .

Conteste las siguientes preguntas en oraciones completas. Cada
oración debe tener un sujeto y un verbo. Comience cada oración
con una mayúscula y termínela con un signo de puntuación.

7. **Do you sleep on a hard or soft bed?**

   _____

8. **Why do you like a hard or soft bed?**

   _____

9. **Do you like to sleep on the top or bottom bunk?**

   _____

10. **Do you have a blanket or a quilt on your bed?**

   _____

Sentence Type * Tipo de oración

Las oraciones pueden ser declaraciones, preguntas, órdenes o exclamaciones. Es necesario reconocer los tipos de oraciones para entender el papel de los signos de puntuación finales, lo cual proporciona una mejor comprensión en la lectura.

Lea la oración y después decida si es una declaración, una pregunta, una orden o una exclamación. Los puntos están al final de las declaraciones y las órdenes. Los signos de interrogación están al final de las preguntas. Los signos de exclamación están al final de las oraciones que demuestran mucho sentimiento o emoción.

Escriba *declaración, orden, pregunta* o *exclamación* después de cada oración.

1. **Put the blue sheets on the bed.** _____

2. **I fed the dog.** _____

3. **Please feed the cat.** _____

4. **Stop!** _____

5. **The shells are on the mat.** _____

6. **Where are your friends?** _____

7. **There are six sleds.** _____

8. **Hush up!** _____

9. **Do not drop the dish.** _____

10. **I had fun at the prom.** _____

11. **What did you say?** _____

12. **Ouch!** _____

Answer Key * Las Respuestas

Fill in the Blanks * Llene el Espacio (page 65)

1. sheet
2. dishes
3. flag
4. mops
5. glasses
6. trash
7. rug
8. brushes
9. pan
10. bed
11. fan
12. clock

Visualizing * Visualización (page 66)

Comprehension * Comprensión (page 68)

1.	in	4.	jump
2.	bunk	5.	under
3.	sheet	6.	sleeping

7. *Answers will vary.*
8. *Answers will vary.*
9. *Answers will vary.*
10. *Answers will vary.*

Sentence Type * Tipo de oración (page 69)

1. command
2. statement
3. command
4. exclamation
5. statement
6. question
7. statement
8. exclamation
9. command
10. statement
11. question
12. exclamation

Lesson 11 * Lección 11

Vocabulary * Vocabulario

Describing Words * Palabras de descripción

Coloque las palabras de vocabulario en inglés en orden alfabético. Para hacerlo, escriba primero las palabras que comienzan con <u>a</u>, luego las que comienzan con <u>b</u>, después <u>c</u>, <u>d</u>, <u>e</u>, y así sucesivamente. Si dos palabras comienzan con la misma letra, entonces considere la siguiente letra y escriba la palabra que tenga la segunda letra más cercana al principio del alfabeto.

English	Spanish	Alphabetize
1. big	grande	1.
2. free	gratis	2.
3. fresh	fresco	3.
4. sick	enfermo	4.
5. slick	resbaladizo	5.
6. flat	plano	6.
7. slim	delgado	7.
8. ten	diez	8.
9. two	dos	9.
10. six	seis	10.
11. wet	mojado	11.
12. sad	triste	12.
13. mad	enojado	13.
14. quick	rápido	14.
15. glad	alegre	15.

Rhyming Words * Palabras que riman

Escriba la palabra del vocabulario que rime con la palabra de rima y luego escriba su propia palabra de rima que corresponda con la palabra del vocabulario. Las palabras que riman son palabras que comienzan de manera diferente pero terminan con la misma vocal y los mismos sonidos en la terminación. Por ejemplo, *red, bed* y *said* son palabras que riman. No necesitan escribirse igual, pero necesitan terminar con la misma vocal y los mismos sonidos en la terminación.

Vocabulary Word	Rhyming Word	Rhyming Word
1. _____	stick	_____
2. _____	trim	_____
3. _____	get	_____
4. _____	had	_____
5. _____	fig	_____
6. _____	bad	_____
7. _____	sat	_____
8. _____	brick	_____
9. _____	tree	_____
10. _____	hen	_____
11. _____	dad	_____
12. _____	fix	_____
13. _____	mesh	_____
14. _____	trick	_____
15. _____	do	_____

Visualizing * Visualización

Visualizar lo que lee le ayudará a recordar lo que ha leído.

Lea cada oración y después dibuje una figura de lo que ve en su mente cuando lee la oración.

The two sad kids are sick in bed.

The mad slim man has a wet hat.

Fluency * Fluidez

Fluidez es la facultad de leer a un ritmo rápido sin detenerse mucho a identificar palabras. Con buena fluidez, una persona puede pensar acerca de lo que está leyendo en lugar de batallar con la pronunciación de las palabras.

Practique leyendo la historia que está a continuación hasta que tenga buena fluidez. Debe poder leer esta historia en menos de un minuto.

Feelings

We have feelings. We can feel glad. We can feel sad. We can feel mad. When you win a prize you feel glad. When you pass a quiz you feel glad. When you cut your leg you feel sad. When you drop your snack you feel sad. When your new truck gets hit you feel mad. When a kid grabs your sled you get mad. Everyone has feelings. Some people say they see red when they get mad. When people feel blue that means they feel sad.

Lea las palabras, primero de arriba a abajo y luego de izquierda a derecha. Practique leyendo las palabras hasta que pueda leerlas sin pausas y a un ritmo rápido.

feel	when	cut
heel	hen	shut
reel	pen	hut
eel	den	but
steel	men	nut

74

Comprehension * Comprensión

Llene los espacios con las palabras correctas de la historia acerca de **Feelings**.

1. **You feel** _____ **when you win a prize.**

2. **You feel** _____ **when you drop your snack.**

3. **You feel** _____ **when someone hits your new truck.**

4. **Some people see** _____ **when they get mad.**

5. **When people are sad they feel** _____ **.**

6. **Everyone has** _____ **.**

Conteste las siguientes preguntas en oraciones completas. Cada oración debe tener un sujeto y un verbo. Comience cada oración con una mayúscula y termínela con un signo de puntuación.

7. **Write a sentence about the last time you felt sad.**

   _____

8. **Write a sentence about the last time you felt mad.**

   _____

9. **Write a sentence about the last time you felt glad.**

   _____

10. **There are many feelings. What's your favorite feeling?**

   _____

Categories * Categorías

Escriba las siguientes palabras en la categoría correcta.

run	beets	van	yellow
truck	blue	red	egg
ham	dig	hop	bus
play	jet	clams	black
green	swim	beef	sled
white	pink	grab	fell
figs	cab	fix	hot dogs
sub	brown	fish	gray
jam	ship	cut	jeep

Action Words	Food	Transportation	Colors

Answer Key * Las Respuestas

Alphabetizing * Colocar en orden alfabético (page 71)

1. big	5. glad	9. sick	13. ten
2. flat	6. mad	10. six	14. two
3. free	7. quick	11. slick	15. wet
4. fresh	8. sad	12. slim	

Rhyming Words * Palabras que riman (page 72)
Rhyming words will vary.

1. quick or sick or slick	6. sad, glad, or mad	11. sad or glad or mad
2. slim	7. flat	12. six
3. wet	8. quick or sick or slick	13. fresh
4. sad or glad or mad	9. free	14. quick or sick or slick
5. big	10. ten	15. two

Visualizing * Visualización (page 73)

Comprehension * Comprensión (page 75)

1. glad	4. red
2. sad	5. blue
3. mad	6. feelings

7. *Answers will vary.*
8. *Answers will vary.*
9. *Answers will vary.*
10. *Answers will vary.*

Categories * Categorías (page 76)

Action Words	Food	Transportation	Colors
run	ham	truck	green
play	figs	sub	white
dig	beets	jet	blue
swim	jam	cab	pink
hop	clams	ship	brown
grab	beef	van	red
fix	fish	bus	yellow
cut	egg	sled	black
fell	hot dogs	jeep	gray

Lesson 12 * Lección 12

Vocabulary * Vocabulario

Plurals * Plurales

pills
píldoras

axes
hachas

rays
rayos

seeds
semillas

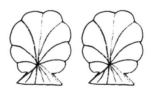

shells
conchas

quizzes
examenes

queens
reinas

spots
manchas

glasses
vasos

locks
candados

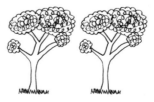

trees
árboles

dresses
vestidos

Fill in the Blanks * Llene el Espacio

Llene cada espacio con una palabra de la página de vocabulario.
Use la figura al final de la oración para ayudarse.

1. I will plant the _____ .

2. The sun's _____ feel good on my skin.

3. Fill the _____ with water.

4. Here are _____ for your lockers.

5. Cut the logs with the _____ .

6. Your _____ are on the dish.

7. I will press the six _____ .

8. We have _____ today in our classes.

9. The socks have red _____ .

10. Where are the _____ ?

11. The _____ will come to the prom.

12. Let's sit under the _____ .

Visualizing * Visualización

Visualizar lo que lee le ayudará a recordar lo que ha leído.

Lea cada oración y después dibuje una figura de lo que ve en su mente cuando lee la oración.

Dad fills four purple glasses with water.

Mom presses the pink dress.

Fluency * Fluidez

Fluidez es la facultad de leer a un ritmo rápido sin detenerse mucho a identificar palabras. Con buena fluidez, una persona puede pensar acerca de lo que está leyendo en lugar de batallar con la pronunciación de las palabras.

Practique leyendo la historia que está a continuación hasta que tenga buena fluidez. Debe poder leer esta historia en menos de un minuto.

Trees

Trees are big plants. Trees have green leaves and brown trunks. Animals live in trees. Birds make nests in trees. Some animals sleep in trees. Trees need water. Trees need air. Trees need sun. Trees are good for us. Trees give us fruit. Figs grow on trees. Trees give us wood. We make many things from wood. Trees give us shade. People like to sit under trees. Kids like to play in trees. Cats like to hide in trees.

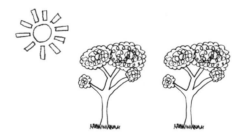

Lea las palabras, primero de arriba a abajo y luego de izquierda a derecha. Practique leyendo las palabras hasta que pueda leerlas sin pausas y a un ritmo rápido.

tree	deep	need
free	sheep	heed
flee	peep	feed
bee	keep	deed
see	beep	reed

Comprehension * Comprensión

Llene los espacios con las palabras correctas de la historia acerca de
Trees.

1. **Trees are big** _____ .

2. **Trees have** _____ **leaves.**

3. **Trees have** _____ **trunks.**

4. **Trees give us fruit and** _____ .

5. **People like to sit** _____ **trees.**

6. **Kids like to play** _____ **trees.**

Conteste las siguientes preguntas en oraciones completas. Cada
oración debe tener un sujeto y un verbo. Comience cada oración
con una mayúscula y termínela con un signo de puntuación.

7. **Name three things trees need.**

   _____

8. **Name a fruit that grows on trees.**

   _____

9. **Name two things we make from wood.**

   _____

10. **Have you ever played in a tree?**

   _____

82

Vowel Sounds * Sonidos vocales

Ordene las imágenes según sus sonidos vocales. En la tabla, escriba el nombre de cada imagen bajo la imagen con el mismo sonido vocal.

Answer Key * Las Respuestas

Fill in the Blanks * Llene el Espacio (page 79)

1. seeds
2. rays
3. glasses
4. locks
5. axes
6. pills
7. dresses
8. quizzes
9. spots
10. shells
11. queens
12. trees

Visualizing * Visualización (page 80)

Comprehension * Comprensión (page 82)

1.	plants	4.	wood
2.	green	5.	under
3.	brown	6.	in

7. Trees need water, air, and sun.
8. Figs grow on trees. *Or answers will vary.*
9. *Answers will vary.*
10. *Answers will vary.*

Vowel Sounds * Sonidos vocales (page 83)

pan	bay	creek	shed
clam	pray	queen	bed
ax	hay	seed	sled
ham	pay	feet	jet

Lesson 13 * Lección 13

Vocabulary * Vocabulario

Words with Multiple Meanings * Palabras con múltiples significados

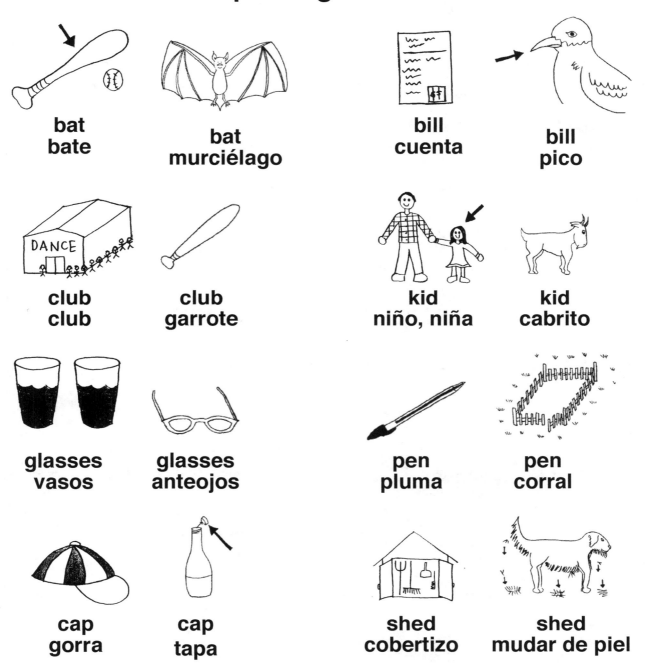

bat
bate

bat
murciélago

bill
cuenta

bill
pico

club
club

club
garrote

kid
niño, niña

kid
cabrito

glasses
vasos

glasses
anteojos

pen
pluma

pen
corral

cap
gorra

cap
tapa

shed
cobertizo

shed
mudar de piel

Fill in the Blanks * Llene el Espacio

Llene cada espacio con una palabra de la página de vocabulario. Use la figura al final de la oración para ayudarse. Lea la oración con cuidado porque puede necesitar añadir una <u>s</u> o las letras <u>es</u> a la palabra del vocabulario.

1. Where are my _____ ?

2. The cop has a _____ on his belt.

3. Did you see the snake _____ its skin?

4. She will hit the ball with the _____ .

5. The cat hid in the _____ .

6. I have two red _____ .

7. The _____ are playing with their trucks.

8. The _____ are sleeping in the grass.

9. The two yellow _____ fell on the floor.

10. The _____ live in the cave.

11. We will have a snack at the _____ .

12. The bird has a sharp _____ .

Visualizing * Visualización

Visualizar lo que lee le ayudará a recordar lo que ha leído.

Lea cada oración y después dibuje una figura de lo que ve en su mente cuando lee la oración.

The bird's bill is long and sharp.

Your dog sheds a lot of hair!

Fluency * Fluidez

Fluidez es la facultad de leer a un ritmo rápido sin detenerse mucho a identificar palabras. Con buena fluidez, una persona puede pensar acerca de lo que está leyendo en lugar de batallar con la pronunciación de las palabras.

Practique leyendo la historia que está a continuación hasta que tenga buena fluidez. Debe poder leer esta historia en menos de un minuto.

A Kid

A kid is a baby goat. A kid likes to play. A kid can jump. A kid can run up a hill. Most kids are twins. They hit their heads together. Kids like to eat. They will nip at your clothes. They nip with their lips. Another kind of kid is a boy or girl. They like to play. They like to jump. Boys and girls can run up a hill. Some boys and girls are twins. Boys and girls like to eat. They will not nip at your clothes like baby goats. Boys and girls like to pet baby goats.

Lea las palabras, primero de arriba a abajo y luego de izquierda a derecha. Practique leyendo las palabras hasta que pueda leerlas sin pausas y a un ritmo rápido.

in	rag	say
fin	brag	stay
grin	tag	play
pin	bag	pay
twin	drag	lay

Comprehension * Comprensión

Llene los espacios con las palabras correctas de la historia acerca de
A Kid.

1. **A kid is a baby** _____ .

2. **Most kids are** _____ .

3. **They hit their** _____ **together.**

4. **Kids like to nip with their** _____ .

5. **Another kind of kid is a boy or** _____ .

6. **Boys and girls like to** _____ **baby goats.**

Conteste las siguientes preguntas en oraciones completas. Cada oración debe tener un sujeto y un verbo. Comience cada oración con una mayúscula y termínela con un signo de puntuación.

7. **Name two things baby goats like to do.**

   _____

8. **Have you ever pet a baby goat?**

   _____

9. **Name three different kinds of kids.**

   _____

10. **What kind of kid likes to nip at clothes?**

   _____

Words With Multiple Meanings
Palabras con múltiples significados

Llene cada espacio con una palabra de la tabla. Use la imagen al final de la oración o la información en la tabla para ayudrarse.

	stick palo		stick adherirse a algo		spot mancha		spot punto, lugar preciso
	back espalda		back regreso		tag etiqueta		tag jugar a la pega
	jam mermelada		jam congestión		cross cruz		cross cruzar

1. There is a green _____ on your dress.

2. The kids play _____ on the grass.

3. Do not hit the dog with the _____ .

4. Give the doll _____ to your sister.

5. Look at the _____ for the price.

6. Look both ways before you _____ the street.

7. Mom puts _____ on the bread.

8. This is a good _____ for a picnic.

9. She wears a _____ around her neck.

10. I will lick the stamp so it will _____ .

11. Our car is in a traffic _____ .

12. There is a bug on your _____ .

Answer Key * Las Respuestas

Fill in the Blanks * Llene el Espacio (page 86)

1.	glasses	7.	kids
2.	club	8.	kids
3.	shed	9.	glasses
4.	bat	10.	bats
5.	shed	11.	club
6.	caps	12.	bill

Visualizing * Visualización (page 87)

 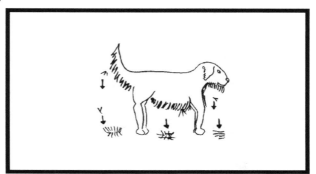

Comprehension * Comprensión (page 89)

1. goat	4. lips
2. twins	5. girl
3. heads	6. pet

7. Baby goats like to play and eat.
8. *Answers will vary.*
9. Three different kinds of kids are baby goats, boys, and girls.
10. Baby goats like to nip at clothes.

Words with Multiple Meanings * Palabras con múltiples significados (page 90)

1.	spot	7.	jam
2.	tag	8.	spot
3.	stick	9.	cross
4.	back	10.	stick
5.	tag	11.	jam
6.	cross	12.	back

Lesson 14 * Lección 14

Vocabulary * Vocabulario

Numbers * Números

1
one
uno

2
two
dos

3
three
tres

4
four
cuatro

5
five
cinco

6
six
seis

7
seven
siete

8
eight
ocho

9
nine
nueve

10
ten
diez

11
eleven
once

12
twelve
doce

Fill in the Blanks * Llene el Espacio

Llene cada espacio con una palabra de la página de vocabulario. Use los números que están al final de la oración para ayudarse.

1. I can hear the _____ children playing. **6**

2. Put the _____ glasses here. **7**

3. I see _____ yellow buses. **10**

4. The _____ blue dishes are on the green mat. **3**

5. I see _____ blue fish in the water. **8**

6. Sam fed _____ deer. **1**

7. Pat will feed _____ deer. **9**

8. _____ kids are on the red sled. **2**

9. Meg met _____ friends at the club. **4**

10. Here are _____ eggs. **12**

11. _____ men are in the orange van. **5**

12. The slim man has _____ pups. **11**

Visualizing * Visualización

Visualizar lo que lee le ayudará a recordar lo que ha leído.

Lea cada oración y después dibuje una figura de lo que ve en su mente cuando lee la oración.

There are five red bugs on the brown log.

The man has two big scabs on his leg.

Fluency * Fluidez

Fluidez es la facultad de leer a un ritmo rápido sin detenerse mucho a identificar palabras. Con buena fluidez, una persona puede pensar acerca de lo que está leyendo en lugar de batallar con la pronunciación de las palabras.

Practique leyendo la historia que está a continuación hasta que tenga buena fluidez. Debe poder leer esta historia en menos de un minuto.

Pets

Sam has many pets. He has two dogs and three cats. One dog had pups. It had six pups. One cat had kittens. It had five kittens. Sam likes animals. He also has fish. He has one blue fish, two yellow fish, and three black fish. Sam likes to take care of his pets. His pets need food. They need water. Sam plays with his pets. The dogs and pups run and play outside. The cats and kittens jump and play inside. Sam will sell the pups. He will sell the kittens. He will find a good home for his pets. He loves his pets.

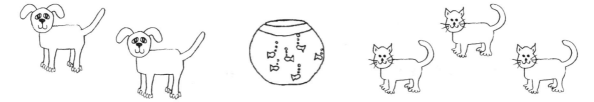

Lea las palabras, primero de arriba a abajo y luego de izquierda a derecha. Practique leyendo las palabras hasta que pueda leerlas sin pausas y a un ritmo rápido.

queen	sick	shop
quit	rock	ship
quick	sack	dish
quack	stick	cash
quiz	shack	shell

Comprehension * Comprensión

Llene los espacios con las palabras correctas de la historia acerca de
Pets.

1. Sam has _____ **dogs.**

2. Sam has _____ **cats.**

3. Sam has one blue _____ .

4. Sam has _____ **black fish.**

5. Sam's dogs like to play _____ .

6. Sam's cats play _____ .

Conteste las siguientes preguntas en oraciones completas. Cada oración debe tener un sujeto y un verbo. Comience cada oración con una mayúscula y termínela con un signo de puntuación.

7. **How many pups did Sam's dog have?**

   _____

8. **How many kittens did Sam's cat have?**

   _____

9. **What will Sam do with the pups and kittens?**

   _____

10. **How many pets do you have?**

    _____

Plurals * Plurales

Use la palabras de la tabla para llenar los espacios. Lea la oración con cuidado ya que puede necesitar añadir una s o las letras es a la palabra.

glass	deer	dress	dish
fish	friend	kiss	box
day	truck	ax	quilt

1. You can meet your _____ at the club.

2. There are four large orange _____ in the water.

3. The men will cut the logs with the three _____ .

4. Stack the ten _____ here.

5. Put the blue and red _____ on the bed.

6. Mom will press the five pink _____ .

7. Put the fish on the three green _____ .

8. I see four brown _____ in the grass.

9. There are seven _____ in a week.

10. Dad puts water in the six yellow _____ .

11. Sam gives the pup a _____ .

12. Tom sits in the purple _____ .

Answer Key * Las Respuestas

Fill in the Blanks * Llene el Espacio (page 93)

1.	six	7.	nine
2.	seven	8.	Two
3.	ten	9.	four
4.	three	10.	twelve
5.	eight	11.	Five
6.	one	12.	eleven

Visualizing * Visualización (page 94)

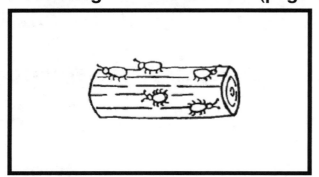

Comprehension * Comprensión (page 96)

1.	two	4.	three
2.	three	5.	outside
3.	fish	6.	inside

7. Sam's dog had six pups.
8. Sam's cat had five kittens.
9. Sam will sell the pups and kittens.
10. *Answers will vary.*

Plurals * Plurales (page 97)

1.	friends	7.	dishes
2.	fish	8.	deer
3.	axes	9.	days
4.	boxes	10.	glasses
5.	quilts	11.	kiss
6.	dresses	12.	truck

Lesson 15 * Lección 15

Vocabulary * Vocabulario

More Things * Más cosas

mat
tapete

pin
alfiler

cup
taza

cash
dinero en efectivo

jug
garrafón

wax
cera

can
lata

tag
etiqueta

bib
babero

tub
bañera

pen
pluma

net
red

Fill in the Blanks * Llene el Espacio

Llene cada espacio con una palabra de la página de vocabulario. Use la figura al final de la oración para ayudarse. Lea la oración con cuidado porque puede necesitar añadir una s o las letras es a la palabra del vocabulario.

1. The pups play on the blue _____ .

2. The _____ say $5.00.

3. Pam has a big fish in the _____ .

4. Here is a _____ of beets.

5. There is jam on the two yellow _____ .

6. Where are the six red _____ ?

7. Here is your pill and a _____ of water.

8. Dad got stuck with a _____ .

9. Mom puts water in the _____ .

10. The _____ is hot!

11. Sam will pay _____ to the man.

12. Fill the five brown _____ with water.

Visualizing * Visualización

Visualizar lo que lee le ayudará a recordar lo que ha leído.

Lea cada oración y después dibuje una figura de lo que ve en su mente cuando lee la oración.

The three yellow pups play on the blue and red mat.

The green tags on the hats say $10.

Fluency * Fluidez

Fluidez es la facultad de leer a un ritmo rápido sin detenerse mucho a identificar palabras. Con buena fluidez, una persona puede pensar acerca de lo que está leyendo en lugar de batallar con la pronunciación de las palabras.

Practique leyendo la historia que está a continuación hasta que tenga buena fluidez. Debe poder leer esta historia en menos de un minuto.

Cash

   Al pays his bills with cash. He pays cash for his food. He pays cash for his clothes. He pays cash for his gas. He keeps his cash in his wallet. When he wants more cash, he goes to the bank. The bank gives him many bills. The bank gives him one-dollar bills. The bank gives him five, ten and twenty-dollar bills. The bills are green. He gets new bills from the bank. Al likes to shop. He likes to shop at the mall. He shops on Saturdays. He gets paid at his job on Fridays.

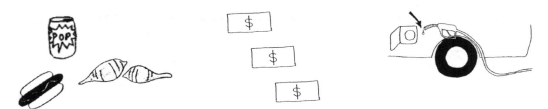

Lea las palabras, primero de arriba a abajo y luego de izquierda a derecha. Practique leyendo las palabras hasta que pueda leerlas sin pausas y a un ritmo rápido.

by	me	stop
my	he	stay
shy	we	step
fly	she	stick
cry	be	stuck

Comprehension * Comprensión

Llene los espacios con las palabras correctas de la historia acerca de **Cash.**

1. **Al pays his bills with** _____ .

2. **Al keeps his cash in his** _____ .

3. **He gets cash at the** _____ .

4. **The bank gives Al many** _____ .

5. **The bills are** _____ .

6. **Al likes to shop at the** _____ .

Conteste las siguientes preguntas en oraciones completas. Cada oración debe tener un sujeto y un verbo. Comience cada oración con una mayúscula y termínela con un signo de puntuación.

7. **Name four bills Al gets at the bank.**

_____

8. **What day does Al get paid?**

_____

9. **What day does Al like to shop?**

_____

10. **Name three things Al pays cash for.**

_____

What's Missing? * ¿Qué falta?

Complete cada oración. Falta el verbo o el sujeto de cada una de las oraciones. Después de cada oración escriba una **S** si faltaba el sujeto o una **V** si faltaba el verbo.

Ejemplo: _____ run in the park.
The kids run in the park.   S

1. _____ **will toss the cap to Bob.** _____

2. **The red _____ is on the bed.** _____

3. **Your _____ can sit on the mat.** _____

4. **Ted _____ the ham.** _____

5. **Pam _____ in the mud.** _____

6. **The fox _____ up the hill.** _____

7. **The _____ sleep in the hay.** _____

8. **_____ pays with cash.** _____

9. **_____ sits on the quilt.** _____

10. **The _____ is stuck in the mud.** _____

11. **The dogs _____ in the grass.** _____

12. **A frog _____ on the mat.** _____

Answer Key * Las Respuestas

Fill in the Blanks * Llene el Espacio (page 100)

1.	mat	7.	cup
2.	tags	8.	pin
3.	net	9.	jug
4.	can	10.	wax
5.	bibs	11.	cash
6.	pens	12.	tubs

Visualizing * Visualización (page 101)

Comprehension * Comprensión (page 103)

1.	cash	4.	bills
2.	wallet	5.	green
3.	bank	6.	mall

7. Al gets one, five, ten, and twenty dollar bills at the bank.
8. Al gets paid on Fridays.
9. Al likes to shop on Saturdays.
10. Al pays cash for food, clothes, and gas.

What's Missing? * ¿Qué falta? (page 104)
Answers will vary except for the S (subject) and V (verb).

1.	Dad, S	7.	cats, S
2.	bell, S	8.	Mom, S
3.	cat, S	9.	Sam, S
4.	smells, V	10.	truck, S
5.	fell, V	11.	play, V
6.	ran, V	12.	sat, V

Lesson 16 * Lección 16

Vocabulary * Vocabulario

Nature * La naturaleza

log
tronco

hay
heno

sun
sol

mud
lodo

seed
semilla

shell
concha

tree
árbol

grass
césped

rock
piedra

bud
botón

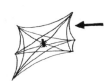

web
telaraña

stick
palo

Fill in the Blanks * Llene el Espacio

Llene cada espacio con una palabra de la página de vocabulario. Use la figura al final de la oración para ayudarse. Lea la oración con cuidado porque puede necesitar añadir una s o las letras es a la palabra del vocabulario.

1. **The bug lays its eggs on a _____ .**

2. **Pam puts the three _____ on the mat.**

3. **It feels good to sit in the _____ .**

4. **Dad cuts the _____ on Sunday.**

5. **There is green moss on the _____ .**

6. **The pups nap in the _____ .**

7. **I see a big bug stuck in the _____ .**

8. **The chicks peck at the _____ .**

9. **Let's sit under the _____ .**

10. **The dogs play in the _____ .**

11. **We will step on the _____ to cross the creek.**

12. **The plant has five _____ .**

107

Visualizing * Visualización

Visualizar lo que lee le ayudará a recordar lo que ha leído.

Lea cada oración y después dibuje una figura de lo que ve en su mente cuando lee la oración.

There is a big purple bug stuck in the web.

In the grass, three yellow chicks peck at the seeds.

Fluency * Fluidez

Fluidez es la facultad de leer a un ritmo rápido sin detenerse mucho a identificar palabras. Con buena fluidez, una persona puede pensar acerca de lo que está leyendo en lugar de batallar con la pronunciación de las palabras.

Practique leyendo la historia que está a continuación hasta que tenga buena fluidez. Debe poder leer esta historia en menos de un minuto.

Seeds

Seeds come from plants. Seeds grow into new plants. Trees grow from seeds. Flowers grow from seeds. Grass grows from seeds. Weeds grow from seeds. Seeds need air, sun, and water to grow. Most seeds grow in soil. Seeds are different sizes. Some seeds are tiny. Other seeds are bigger. Some seeds are black. Other seeds are white. You can buy seeds at a shop. Farmers plant seeds in the spring. The seeds grow into plants. The plants grow in the spring and summer. Crops are ready to be picked in the summer and fall.

Lea las palabras, primero de arriba a abajo y luego de izquierda a derecha. Practique leyendo las palabras hasta que pueda leerlas sin pausas y a un ritmo rápido.

pass	bell	off
boss	gull	puff
less	shell	fuzz
miss	hill	jazz
toss	doll	buzz

Comprehension * Comprensión

Llene los espacios con las palabras correctas de la historia acerca de
Seeds.

1. **Seeds come from** _____ .

2. **Grass** _____ **from seeds.**

3. **Seeds need air, sun, and** _____ .

4. **Most seeds grow in** _____ .

5. **Farmers plant seeds in the** _____ .

6. **Crops are ready to be** _____ **in the spring and summer.**

Conteste las siguientes preguntas en oraciones completas. Cada
oración debe tener un sujeto y un verbo. Comience cada oración
con una mayúscula y termínela con un signo de puntuación.

7. **What color are seeds?**

   _____

8. **Name three plants that grow from seeds.**

   _____

9. **Who plants seeds in the spring?**

   _____

10. **What plant do people not want in their garden?**

   _____

110

Vowel Sounds * Sonidos vocales

Ordene las imágenes según sus sonidos vocales. En la tabla, escriba el nombre de cada imagen bajo la imagen con el mismo sonido vocal.

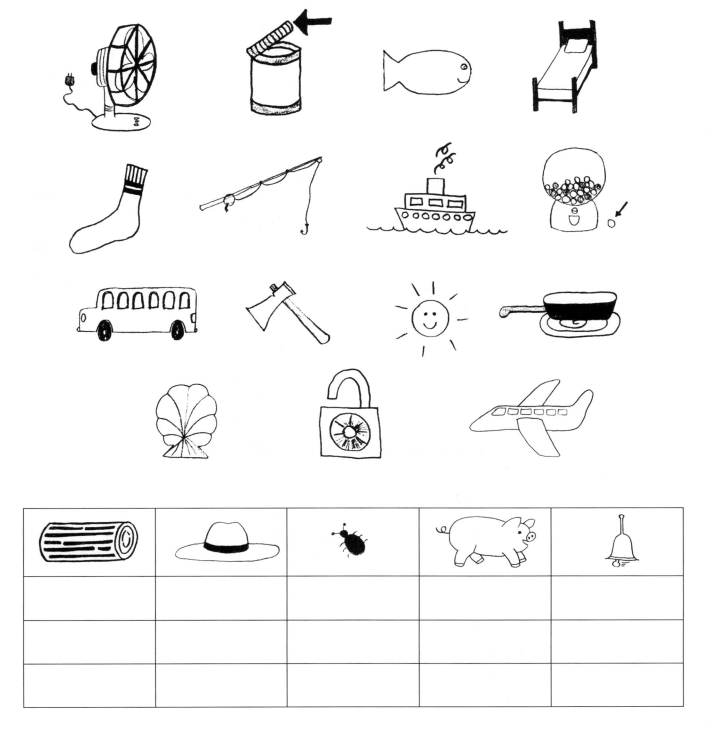

Answer Key * Las Respuestas

Fill in the Blanks * Llene el Espacio (page 107)

1. stick
2. shells
3. sun
4. grass
5. log
6. hay
7. web
8. seeds
9. tree
10. mud
11. rock
12. buds

Visualizing * Visualización (page 108)

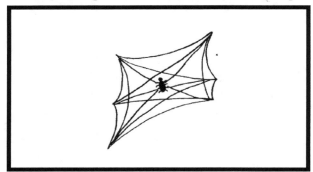

Comprehension * Comprensión (page 110)

1.	plants	4.	soil
2.	grows	5.	spring
3.	water	6.	picked

7. Seeds are black or white.
8. Trees, flowers, and grass grow from seeds.
9. Farmers plant seeds in the spring.
10. People do not want weeds in their garden.

Vowel Sounds * Sonidos vocales (page 111)

sock	fan	gum	lid	bed
rod	ax	bus	fish	shell
lock	pan	sun	ship	jet

Lesson 17 * Lección 17

Vocabulary * Vocabulario

More Action Words * Más palabras de acción

Coloque las palabras de vocabulario en inglés en orden alfabético. Para hacerlo, escriba primero las palabras que comienzan con <u>a</u>, luego las que comienzan con <u>b</u>, después <u>c</u>, <u>d</u>, <u>e</u>, y así sucesivamente. Si dos palabras comienzan con la misma letra, entonces considere la siguiente letra y escriba la palabra que tenga la segunda letra más cercana al principio del alfabeto.

English	Spanish
1. mix	mezclar
2. pray	rezar
3. hug	abrazar
4. pay	pagar
5. kiss	besar
6. pick	recoger
7. hop	saltar
8. play	jugar
9. meet	encontrar
10. pack	empacar
11. mop	trapear
12. pass	pasar
13. jog	trotar
14. run	correr

Alphabetize
1.
2.
3.
4.
5.
6.
7.
8.
9.
10.
11.
12.
13.
14.

Fill in the Blanks * Llene el Espacio

Llene cada espacio con una palabra de la página de vocabulario. Use la figura al final de la oración para ayudarse. Lea la oración con cuidado porque puede necesitar añadir una s o las letras es a la palabra del vocabulario.

1. Sam can _____ on one leg.

2. Pat and Sal will _____ at the club.

3. Jim will _____ his bags for the trip.

4. Bob gives Mom a _____ .

5. Dad will _____ the figs off the tree.

6. Pam _____ up the hill.

7. Meg gives the dog two _____ .

8. Dad _____ for the truck with cash.

9. The kids _____ on the hill.

10. Pam _____ the water and mud in a cup.

11. Kim _____ the ball to Alex.

12. Bill _____ every day.

Visualizing * Visualización

Visualizar lo que lee le ayudará a recordar lo que ha leído.

Lea cada oración y después dibuje una figura de lo que ve en su mente cuando lee la oración.

Sam can hop on one leg.

Dad picks figs off the tree.

Fluency * Fluidez

Fluidez es la facultad de leer a un ritmo rápido sin detenerse mucho a identificar palabras. Con buena fluidez, una persona puede pensar acerca de lo que está leyendo en lugar de batallar con la pronunciación de las palabras.

Practique leyendo la historia que está a continuación hasta que tenga buena fluidez. Debe poder leer esta historia en menos de un minuto.

Fun

Kids like to have fun. They like to run in the sun. They like to swim in a lake. They like to mix water and mud to make mud cakes. It is fun to sit on a rug and play. It is fun to hug your dog. It is fun to kiss your cat. People like to have fun. They meet at a club to have fun. They pay cash to have fun. They may go see a baseball game or football game to have fun. Some people go on a trip to have fun. They pack their bags and then go somewhere. What do you like to do to have fun?

Lea las palabras, primero de arriba a abajo y luego de izquierda a derecha. Practique leyendo las palabras hasta que pueda leerlas sin pausas y a un ritmo rápido.

smash	speck	snag
smell	speed	snack
smock	spell	snap
smog	spin	snip
smack	spit	snug

Comprehension * Comprensión

Llene los espacios con las palabras correctas de la historia acerca de
Fun.

1. **Kids like to have** _____ .

2. **They like to** _____ **in a lake.**

3. **Kids like to** _____ **water and mud.**

4. **It is fun to** _____ **on a rug and play.**

5. **People** _____ **cash to have fun.**

6. **Some people go on a** _____ **to have fun.**

7. **They** _____ **their bags and go somewhere.**

Conteste las siguientes preguntas en oraciones completas. Cada
oración debe tener un sujeto y un verbo. Comience cada oración
con una mayúscula y termínela con un signo de puntuación.

8. **What do you do to have fun?**

   _____

9. **Where do you go to have fun?**

   _____

10. **How much do you pay to have fun?**

    _____

Action Words * Palabras de acción

Escriba la palabra correcta de acción bajo cada figura.

1. _____

2. _____

3. _____

4. _____

5. _____

6. _____

7. _____

8. _____

9. _____

10. _____

11. _____

12. _____

run

dig

hop

mix

pay

hug

meet

jog

kiss

fell

pray

slip

Answer Key * Las Respuestas

Alphabetizing * Colocar en orden alfabético (page 113)

1. hop	5. meet	9. pass	13. pray
2. hug	6. mix	10. pay	14. run
3. jog	7. mop	11. pick	
4. kiss	8. pack	12. play	

Fill in the Blanks * Llene el Espacio (page 114)

1. hop
2. meet
3. pack
4. hug
5. pick
6. jogs or runs
7. kisses
8. pays
9. play
10. mixes
11. passes
12. jogs or runs

Visualizing * Visualización (page 115)

Comprehension * Comprensión (page 117)

1. fun		5. pay	
2. swim		6. trip	
3. mix		7. pack	
4. sit			

8. *Answers will vary.*
9. *Answers will vary.*
10. *Answers will vary.*

Action Words * Palabras de acción (page 118)

1. hop
2. jog or run
3. meet
4. hug
5. kiss
6. cash
7. jog or run
8. dig
9. fell
10. slip
11. pray
12. mix

Lesson 18 * Lección 18

Vocabulary * Vocabulario

More Action Words * Más palabras de acción

Coloque las palabras de vocabulario en inglés en orden alfabético. Para hacerlo, escriba primero las palabras que comienzan con a, luego las que comienzan con b, después c, d, e, y así sucesivamente. Si dos palabras comienzan con la misma letra, entonces considere la siguiente letra y escriba la palabra que tenga la segunda letra más cercana al principio del alfabeto.

English	Spanish		Alphabetize
1. smell	oler		1.
2. see	ver		2.
3. nap	siesta		3.
4. spit	escupir		4.
5. sit	sentar		5.
6. yell	gritar		6.
7. sneeze	estornudar		7.
8. win	ganar		8.
9. smash	aplastar		9.
10. swim	nadar		10.
11. slip	resbalar		11.
12. sweep	barrer		12.
13. sell	vener		13.
14. shut	cerrar		14.

120

Fill in the Blanks * Llene el Espacio

Llene cada espacio con una palabra de la página de vocabulario. Use la figura al final de la oración para ayudarse. Lea la oración con cuidado porque puede necesitar añadir una <u>s</u> o las letras <u>es</u> a la palabra del vocabulario.

1. The kids _____ on the green and red rug.

2. Sam _____ figs at his shop.

3. Dad _____ after lunch.

4. Do not _____ the seeds in the hut.

5. I _____ ham and eggs.

6. Let's _____ at the lake.

7. Pam _____ three cats in the tree.

8. Tom _____ on the ice.

9. Did you _____ the race?

10. The thin man _____ at his dog.

11. Please _____ the door.

12. Do not _____ on the food.

Visualizing * Visualización

Visualizar lo que lee le ayudará a recordar lo que ha leído.

Lea cada oración y después dibuje una figura de lo que ve en su mente cuando lee la oración.

The black and white cat naps on a red mat in the sun.

Ted and his dog swim in the lake.

Fluency * Fluidez

Fluidez es la facultad de leer a un ritmo rápido sin detenerse mucho a identificar palabras. Con buena fluidez, una persona puede pensar acerca de lo que está leyendo en lugar de batallar con la pronunciación de las palabras.

Practique leyendo la historia que está a continuación hasta que tenga buena fluidez. Debe poder leer esta historia en menos de un minuto.

A Dock

A dock sits on top of the water. You can do a lot at a dock. You can sit in the sun. You can fish from a dock. You can swim to a dock. Boats stop at the dock. People lock their boats at the dock. Docks are made of wood. Docks can be on a lake. Docks can be on the ocean. Docks can be on a river. Docks can be long. Docks can be square. There can be shops on a dock. Docks are a fun place.

Lea las palabras, primero de arriba a abajo y luego de izquierda a derecha. Practique leyendo las palabras hasta que pueda leerlas sin pausas y a un ritmo rápido.

swim	black	clap
swam	bleed	class
sweep	block	clip
sweet	blush	clock
swish	bless	clay

Comprehension * Comprensión

Llene los espacios con las palabras correctas de la historia acerca de
A Dock.

1. **A dock** _____ **on the water.**

2. **Boats** _____ **at a dock.**

3. **People** _____ **their boats at a dock.**

4. **Docks are made of** _____ **.**

5. **Docks can be long or** _____ **.**

6. **There can be** _____ **on a dock.**

7. **Docks are a** _____ **place.**

Conteste las siguientes preguntas en oraciones completas. Cada
oración debe tener un sujeto y un verbo. Comience cada oración
con una mayúscula y termínela con un signo de puntuación.

8. **Name three things you can do at a dock.**

   _____

9. **Name three places you can find a dock.**

   _____

10. **What did you do on a dock?**

   _____

Action Words * Palabras de acción

Escriba la palabra correcta de acción bajo cada figura.

1. _____

2. _____

3. _____

4. _____

5. _____

6. _____

7. _____

8. _____

9. _____

10. _____

11. _____

12. _____

sweep

swim

sit

nap

sell

yell

smell

smash

spin

clap

sneeze

flee

Answer Key * Las Respuestas

Alphabetizing * Colocar en orden alfabético (page 120)

1. nap	5. sit	9. sneeze	13. win
2. see	6. slip	10. spit	14. yell
3. sell	7. smash	11. sweep	
4. shut	8. smell	12. swim	

Fill in the Blanks * Llene el Espacio (page 121)

1. sit
2. sells
3. naps
4. spit
5. smell
6. swim
7. sees
8. slips
9. win
10. yells
11. shut
12. sneeze

Visualizing * Visualización (page 122)

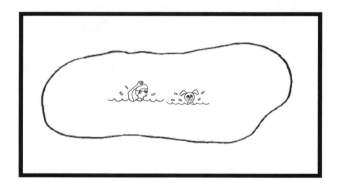

Comprehension * Comprensión (page 124)

1. sits		5. square	
2. stop		6. shops	
3. lock		7. fun	
4. wood			

8. You can sit in the sun, fish and swim at a dock.
9. You can find a dock on a lake, ocean, or river.
10. *Answers will vary.*

Action Words * Palabras de acción (page 125)

1. smash
2. flee
3. sell
4. sneeze
5. smell
6. spin
7. sweep
8. yell
9. swim
10. sit
11. clap
12. nap

Lesson 19 * Lección 19

Vocabulary * Vocabulario

More Animals * Más animales

bat
murciélago

pup
cachorro

duck
pato

kid
cabrito

slug
babosa

hog
cerdo

cub
cachorro

cod
bacalao

gull
gaviota

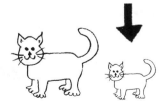

kitten
gatito

frog
rana

flock
bandada

Fill in the Blanks * Llene el Espacio

Llene cada espacio con una palabra de la página de vocabulario. Use la figura al final de la oración para ayudarse. Lea la oración con cuidado porque puede necesitar añadir una <u>s</u> o las letras <u>es</u> a la palabra del vocabulario.

1. The _____ play and run in the grass.

2. Do not step on the _____ .

3. A big green _____ sits on the log.

4. From the dock, I can see a big _____ in the water.

5. The _____ got your chips.

6. That black _____ is fat!

7. Sam will pet the brown and white _____ .

8. Sam will feed the two _____ .

9. _____ have webbed feet.

10. The _____ sleep in a den.

11. A _____ of ducks are on top of the shack.

12. The _____ sleep in a cave.

Visualizing * Visualización

Visualizar lo que lee le ayudará a recordar lo que ha leído.

Lea cada oración y después dibuje una figura de lo que ve en su mente cuando lee la oración.

The gulls got the chips from the bag.

The brown cub ate the bass.

Fluency * Fluidez

Fluidez es la facultad de leer a un ritmo rápido sin detenerse mucho a identificar palabras. Con buena fluidez, una persona puede pensar acerca de lo que está leyendo en lugar de batallar con la pronunciación de las palabras.

Practique leyendo la historia que está a continuación hasta que tenga buena fluidez. Debe poder leer esta historia en menos de un minuto.

Foxes

A baby fox is a pup. A baby fox cannot see. A baby fox cannot hear. It sleeps a lot. It sleeps in a den. The den may be a log. It lives with its mom and dad. Its mom is a vixen. Its dad is a dog fox. Baby foxes suck milk from their mother. Baby foxes are gray and black. Adult foxes are red and brown. In six weeks the baby foxes leave the den. They look around. They learn to hunt. They eat bugs. They eat berries. Mom teaches them to hunt and be safe.

Lea las palabras, primero de arriba a abajo y luego de izquierda a derecha. Practique leyendo las palabras hasta que pueda leerlas sin pausas y a un ritmo rápido.

flat	play	glad
flash	plan	glass
flock	plug	glob
floss	plot	gloss
flesh	plus	glum

Comprehension * Comprensión

Llene los espacios con las palabras correctas de la historia acerca de **Foxes.**

1. **Baby foxes are called** _____ .

2. **Baby foxes sleep in a** _____ .

3. **A mother fox is a** _____ .

4. **The father fox is a** _____ **fox.**

5. **Baby foxes are** _____ **and black.**

6. **Adult foxes are red and** _____ .

7. **In six** _____ **the baby foxes leave the den.**

8. **Baby foxes eat berries and** _____ .

Conteste las siguientes preguntas en oraciones completas. Cada oración debe tener un sujeto y un verbo. Comience cada oración con una mayúscula y termínela con un signo de puntuación.

9. **What are baby dogs called?**

_____

10. **What are baby cats called?**

_____

11. **What are baby goats called?**

_____

Vocabulary * Vocabulario

Llene la tabla con el nombre del animal. Luego coloque una X en cada columna que se aplique a ese animal.

1.
2.
3.
4.
5.
6.
7.
8.
9.
10.
11.
12.

Animal	Swims Nada	Flies Vuela	Fur/Hair Piel/Pelo	Feathers Plumas
1.				
2.				
3.				
4.				
5.				
6.				
7.				
8.				
9.				
10.				
11.				
12.				

132

Answer Key * Las Respuestas

Fill in the Blanks * Llene el Espacio (page 128)

1.	kids	7.	kitten
2.	slug	8.	pups
3.	frog	9.	Ducks
4.	cod	10.	cubs
5.	gulls	11.	flock
6.	hog	12.	bats

Visualizing * Visualización (page 129)

Comprehension * Comprensión (page 131)

1.	pups	5.	gray
2.	den	6.	brown
3.	vixen	7.	weeks
4.	dog	8.	bugs

9. Baby dogs are called pups.
10. Baby cats are called kittens.
11. Baby goats are called kids.

Vocabulary * Vocabulario (page 132)

Animal	Swims	Flies	Fur/Hair	Feathers
1. frog	X			
2. duck	X	X		X
3. deer			X	
4. rat			X	
5. cat			X	
6. pig			X	
7. bee		X		
8. dog	X		X	
9. bat		X	X	
10. cub	X		X	
11. bass	X			
12. gull		X		X

Lesson 20 * Lección 20

Vocabulary * Vocabulario

Sound Words * Palabras que imitan sonidos

Coloque las palabras de vocabulario en inglés en orden alfabético. Para hacerlo, escriba primero las palabras que comienzan con <u>a</u>, luego las que comienzan con <u>b</u>, después <u>c</u>, <u>d</u>, <u>e</u>, y así sucesivamente. Si dos palabras comienzan con la misma letra, entonces considere la siguiente letra y escriba la palabra que tenga la segunda letra más cercana al principio del alfabeto.

English	Spanish	Alphabetize
1. pop	reventar	1.
2. hum	susurrar	2.
3. beep	pitar	3.
4. peep	piar	4.
5. cluck	cloquear	5.
6. buzz	zumbar	6.
7. jazz	tocar con ritmo	7.
8. tick	hacer tictac	8.
9. quack	hacer cua cua	9.
10. swish	agitar el aire	10.
11. slam	azotar	11.
12. crack	chasquear	12.
13. creak	crujir	13.
14. bray	rebuznar	14.

Fill in the Blanks * Llene el Espacio

Llene cada espacio con una palabra de la página de vocabulario. Use la figura al final de la oración para ayudarse. Lea la oración con cuidado porque puede necesitar añadir una s o las letras es a la palabra del vocabulario.

1. The floor _____ .

2. The ducks _____ .

3. Do not _____ the door.

4. The bees _____ .

5. The balloon _____ .

6. The big kid _____ in class.

7. Meg will _____ the horn.

8. Hens _____ and peck.

9. The donkey _____ .

10. Sam can _____ his knuckles.

11. The clock goes _____ tock.

12. The chicks _____ .

13. Dad listens to _____ .

14. The trees _____ in the wind.

Visualizing * Visualización

Visualizar lo que lee le ayudará a recordar lo que ha leído.

Lea cada oración y después dibuje una figura de lo que ve en su mente cuando lee la oración.

The bees buzz in the pink flowers.

The ducks swim and quack in the pond.

Fluency * Fluidez

Fluidez es la facultad de leer a un ritmo rápido sin detenerse mucho a identificar palabras. Con buena fluidez, una persona puede pensar acerca de lo que está leyendo en lugar de batallar con la pronunciación de las palabras.

Practique leyendo la historia que está a continuación hasta que tenga buena fluidez. Debe poder leer esta historia en menos de un minuto.

Sounds

If you go to a farm, you will hear many sounds. The chicks peep. The hens cluck. The ducks quack. The donkeys bray. The pigs grunt. The little dogs yip. The farmer hums or maybe he listens to jazz. Sounds can make us feel good. Some sounds can scare us. The pop of a balloon can scare us. The buzz of a bee scares some people. Some sounds keep us awake. The ticking of a clock can keep people awake. Water dripping can keep people awake. There are sounds all around us. What sounds do you hear right now?

Lea las palabras, primero de arriba a abajo y luego de izquierda a derecha. Practique leyendo las palabras hasta que pueda leerlas sin pausas y a un ritmo rápido.

slam	creek	truck
sled	crack	tray
slick	crib	trip
slim	crop	trash
slip	crash	trick

Comprehension * Comprensión

Llene los espacios con las palabras correctas de la historia acerca de
Sounds.

1. **The chicks** _____ .

2. **The hens** _____ .

3. **The ducks** _____ .

4. **The farmer may hum or listen to** _____ .

5. **Sounds can make us** _____ **good.**

6. **The bees** _____ .

7. **The clocks** _____ .

Conteste las siguientes preguntas en oraciones completas. Cada
oración debe tener un sujeto y un verbo. Comience cada oración
con una mayúscula y termínela con un signo de puntuación.

8. **Name three sounds you can hear on a farm.**

    _____

9. **What sound keeps you awake at night?**

    _____

10. **What sounds do you hear right now?**

    _____

Sounds * Sonidos

Escribe la palabra correcta de sonido bajo cada figura.

1. _____

2. _____

3. _____

4. _____

5. _____

6. _____

7. _____

8. _____

9. _____

10. _____

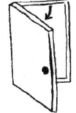

11. _____

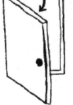

12. _____

pop
hum
peep
cluck
buzz
jazz
tick
quack
swish
bray
creek
crack

Answer Key * Las Respuestas

Alphabetizing * Colocar en orden alfabético (page 134)

1. beep	5. crack	9. peep	13. swish
2. bray	6. creak	10. pop	14. tick
3. buzz	7. hum	11. quack	
4. cluck	8. jazz	12. slam	

Fill in the Blanks * Llene el Espacio (page 135)

1. creaks
2. quack
3. slam
4. buzz
5. pops
6. hums
7. beep
8. cluck
9. brays
10. crack
11. tick
12. peep
13. jazz
14. swish

Visualizing * Visualización (page 136)

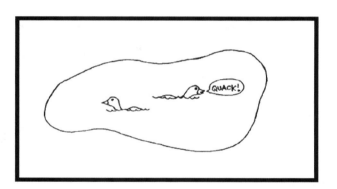

Comprehension * Comprensión (page 138)

1. peep	5. feel
2. cluck	6. buzz
3. quack	7. tick
4. jazz	

8. *Answers will vary.*
9. *Answers will vary.*
10. *Answers will vary.*

Sound Words * Sonidos (page 139)

1. buzz
2. jazz
3. quack
4. swish
5. tick
6. bray
7. cluck
8. peep
9. hum
10. pop
11. creak
12. crack

English Translation of Spanish Directions

Lesson 1

Page 2: Fill in each blank with a word from the vocabulary page. Use the picture at the end of the sentence to help you. Read the sentence carefully because you may need to add <u>s</u> or <u>es</u> to the vocabulary word.

Page 3: Visualizing what you read will help you remember what you have read. **Read** each sentence then draw a picture of what you see in your mind when you read the sentence.

Page 4: Fluency is the ability to read at a fast pace without stopping much to identify words. With good fluency, a person can think about what he/she is reading instead of struggling with sounding out words. **Practice** reading the story below until you have good fluency. You should be able to read this story in less than a minute. **Read** the words, first going down the columns and then across. Practice reading the words until you can read them smoothly and at a fast pace.

Page 5: Fill in the blanks with the correct words from the story about *Pigs*. **Answer** the following questions in complete sentences. Each sentence must have a subject and a verb. Start each sentence with a capital letter and end it with a punctuation mark.

Page 6: Alphabetize the words for the pictures below. Alphabetizing means to put the words in ABC order. First, write all the <u>a</u> words, then the <u>b</u>, then <u>c</u>, <u>d</u>, <u>e</u>, and so forth. If two words begin with the same letter then look at the next letter and write the word which has the second letter closest to the beginning of the alphabet.

Lesson 2

Page 9: Fill in each blank with a word from the vocabulary page. Use the picture at the end of the sentence to help you. Read the sentence carefully because you may need to add <u>s</u> or <u>es</u> to the vocabulary word.

Page 10: Visualizing what you read will help you remember what you have read. **Read** each sentence then draw a picture of what you see in your mind when you read the sentence.

Page 11: Fluency is the ability to read at a fast pace without stopping much to identify words. With good fluency, a person can think about what he/she is reading instead of struggling with sounding out words. **Practice** reading the story below until you have good fluency. You should be able to read this story in less than a minute. **Read** the words, first going down the columns and then across. Practice reading the words until you can read them smoothly and at a fast pace.

Page 12: Fill in the blanks with the correct words from the story about *The Vet*. **Answer** the following questions in complete sentences. Each sentence must have a subject and a verb. Start each sentence with a capital letter and end it with a punctuation mark.

Page 13: Rhyming words are words that begin differently but end with the same vowel and ending sounds. For example, *red, bed,* and *said* are rhyming words. They do not need to be spelled the same, but they do need to end with the same vowel and ending sounds. **Write** the words for the pictures under the correct rime.

Lesson 3

Page 16: Fill in each blank with a word from the vocabulary page. Use the picture at the end of the sentence to help you. Read the sentence carefully because you may need to add <u>s</u> or <u>es</u> to the vocabulary word.

Page 17: Visualizing what you read will help you remember what you have read. **Read** each sentence then draw a picture of what you see in your mind when you read the sentence.

Page 18: Fluency is the ability to read at a fast pace without stopping much to identify words. With good fluency, a person can think about what he/she is reading instead of struggling with sounding out words. **Practice** reading the story below until you have good fluency. You should be able to read this story in less than a minute. **Read** the words, first going down the columns and then across. Practice reading the words until you can read them smoothly and at a fast pace.

Page 19: Fill in the blanks with the correct words from the story about *The Reef*. **Answer** the following questions in complete sentences. Each sentence must have a subject and a verb. Start each sentence with a capital letter and end it with a punctuation mark.

Page 20: Fill in the vowels. The vowels are <u>a</u>, <u>e</u>, <u>i</u>, <u>o</u>, <u>u</u> and sometimes <u>y</u>. Every word or syllable needs a vowel sound.

Lesson 4

Page 23: Fill in each blank with a word from the vocabulary page. Use the picture at the end of the sentence to help you. Read the sentence carefully because you may need to add <u>s</u> or <u>es</u> to the vocabulary word.

Page 24: Visualizing what you read will help you remember what you have read. **Read** each sentence then draw a picture of what you see in your mind when you read the sentence.

Page 25: Fluency is the ability to read at a fast pace without stopping much to identify words. With good fluency, a person can think about what he/she is reading instead of struggling with sounding out words. **Practice** reading the story below until you have good fluency. You should be able to read this story in less than a minute. **Read** the words, first going down the columns and then across. Practice reading the words until you can read them smoothly and at a fast pace.

Page 26: Fill in the blanks with the correct words from the story about *Drums*. **Answer** the following questions in complete sentences. Each sentence must have a subject and a verb. Start each sentence with a capital letter and end it with a punctuation mark.

Page 27: Write the name of each picture in the correct category.

Lesson 5

Page 29: Alphabetize the English vocabulary words. To alphabetize, write all the <u>a</u> words first, then the <u>b</u>, then <u>c</u>, <u>d</u>, <u>e</u>, and so forth. If two words begin with the same letter then look at the next letter and write the word which has the second letter closest to the beginning of the alphabet.

Page 30: Fill in each blank with a word from the vocabulary page. Use the picture at the end of the sentence to help you. Read the sentence carefully because you may need to add <u>s</u> or <u>es</u> to the vocabulary word.

Page 31: Visualizing what you read will help you remember what you have read. **Read** each sentence then draw a picture of what you see in your mind when you read the sentence.

Page 32: Fluency is the ability to read at a fast pace without stopping much to identify words. With good fluency, a person can think about what he/she is reading instead of struggling with sounding out words. **Practice** reading the story below until you have good fluency. You should be able to read this story in less than a minute. **Read** the words, first going down the columns and then across. Practice reading the words until you can read them smoothly and at a fast pace.

Page 33: Fill in the blanks with the correct words from the story about *Play*. **Answer** the following questions in complete sentences. Each sentence must have a subject and a verb. Start each sentence with a capital letter and end it with a punctuation mark.

Page 34: Rhyming words are words that begin differently but end with the same vowel and ending sounds. For example, *red*, *bed*, and *said* are rhyming words. They do not need to be spelled the same, but they do need to end with the same vowel and ending sounds. **Write** two words that rhyme with each vocabulary word.

Lesson 6

Page 37: Fill in each blank with a word from the vocabulary page. Use the picture at the end of the sentence to help you. Read the sentence carefully because you may need to add <u>s</u> or <u>es</u> to the vocabulary word.

Page 38: Visualizing what you read will help you remember what you have read. **Read** each sentence then draw a picture of what you see in your mind when you read the sentence.

Page 39: Fluency is the ability to read at a fast pace without stopping much to identify words. With good fluency, a person can think about what he/she is reading instead of struggling with sounding out words. **Practice** reading the story below until you have good fluency. You should be able to read this story in less than a minute. **Read** the words, first going down the columns and then across. Practice reading the words until you can read them smoothly and at a fast pace.

Page 40: Fill in the blanks with the correct words from the story about *Food*. **Answer** the following questions in complete sentences. Each sentence must have a subject and a verb. Start each sentence with a capital letter and end it with a punctuation mark.

Page 41: Alphabetize the words for the pictures below. Alphabetizing means to put the words in ABC order. The <u>a</u> words will come first (if there are any) then the <u>b</u> words, followed by the <u>c</u>, then <u>d</u>, then <u>f</u> words until all the words have been put in alphabetical order. If there are two words that begin with the same letter then look at the next letter and write the word which has the second letter closest to the beginning of the alphabet.

Lesson 7

Page 44: Fill in each blank with a word from the vocabulary page. Use the picture at the end of the sentence to help you. Read the sentence carefully because you may need to add <u>s</u> or <u>es</u> to the vocabulary word.

Page 45: Visualizing what you read will help you remember what you have read. **Read** each sentence then draw a picture of what you see in your mind when you read the sentence.

Page 46: Fluency is the ability to read at a fast pace without stopping much to identify words. With good fluency, a person can think about what he/she is reading instead of struggling with sounding out words. **Practice** reading the story below until you have good fluency. You should be able to read this story in less than a minute. **Read** the words, first going down the columns and then across. Practice reading the words until you can read them smoothly and at a fast pace.

Page 47: Fill in the blanks with the correct words from the story about *A Sub*. **Answer** the following questions in complete sentences. Each sentence must have a subject and a verb. Start each sentence with a capital letter and end it with a punctuation mark.

Page 48: Fill in the vowels. The vowels are <u>a</u>, <u>e</u>, <u>i</u>, <u>o</u>, <u>u</u> and sometimes <u>y</u>. Every word or syllable needs a vowel sound.

Lesson 8

Page 50: Alphabetize the English vocabulary words. To alphabetize, write all the <u>a</u> words first, then the <u>b</u>, then <u>c</u>, <u>d</u>, <u>e</u>, and so forth. If two words begin with the same letter then look at the next letter and write the word which has the second letter closest to the beginning of the alphabet. The last three words in the list are high frequency sight words.

Page 51: **Write** a vocabulary word that rhymes with each word in the list below. Rhyming words are words that begin differently but end with the same vowel and ending sounds. For example, *red*, *bed*, and *said* are rhyming words. They do not need to be spelled the same, but they do need to end with the same vowel and ending sounds. **Color** each circle the correct color.

Page 52: Visualizing what you read will help you remember what you have read. **Read** each sentence then draw a picture of what you see in your mind when you read the sentence.

Page 53: Fluency is the ability to read at a fast pace without stopping much to identify words. With good fluency, a person can think about what he/she is reading instead of struggling with sounding out words. **Practice** reading the story below until you have good fluency. You should be able to read this story in less than a minute. **Read** the words, first going down the columns and then across. Practice reading the words until you can read them smoothly and at a fast pace.

Page 54: Fill in the blanks with the correct words from the story about *Colors*. **Answer** the following questions in complete sentences. Each sentence must have a subject and a verb. Start each sentence with a capital letter and end it with a punctuation mark.

Page 55: Rearrange the words to make a complete sentence. Start by finding the main action word (verb) and then putting words together to make phrases.

Lesson 9

Page 58: Fill in each blank with a word from the vocabulary page. Use the picture at the end of the sentence to help you. Read the sentence carefully because you may need to add s or es to the vocabulary word.

Page 59: Visualizing what you read will help you remember what you have read. **Read** each sentence then draw a picture of what you see in your mind when you read the sentence.

Page 60: Fluency is the ability to read at a fast pace without stopping much to identify words. With good fluency, a person can think about what he/she is reading instead of struggling with sounding out words. **Practice** reading the story below until you have good fluency. You should be able to read this story in less than a minute. **Read** the words, first going down the columns and then across. Practice reading the words until you can read them smoothly and at a fast pace.

Page 61: Fill in the blanks with the correct words from the story about *Caps*. **Answer** the following questions in complete sentences. Each sentence must have a subject and a verb. Start each sentence with a capital letter and end it with a punctuation mark.

Page 62: Complete each sentence. The verb or subject part of the sentence is missing. After each sentence write **S** if the subject was missing or **V** if the verb was missing.

Example: _____ run in the park.

The kids run in the park. S

Lesson 10

Page 65: Fill in each blank with a word from the vocabulary page. Use the picture at the end of the sentence to help you. Read the sentence carefully because you may need to add s or es to the vocabulary word.

Page 66: Visualizing what you read will help you remember what you have read. **Read** each sentence then draw a picture of what you see in your mind when you read the sentence.

Page 67: Fluency is the ability to read at a fast pace without stopping much to identify words. With good fluency, a person can think about what he/she is reading instead of struggling with sounding out words. **Practice** reading the story below until you have good fluency. You should be able to read this story in less than a minute. **Read** the words, first going down the columns and then across. Practice reading the words until you can read them smoothly and at a fast pace.

Page 68: Fill in the blanks with the correct words from the story about *Beds*. **Answer** the following questions in complete sentences. Each sentence must have a subject and a verb. Start each sentence with a capital letter and end it with a punctuation mark.

Page 69: Sentences may be statements, questions, commands, or exclamations. Recognizing sentence types is necessary for understanding the role of end punctuation which provides for better reading comprehension. **Read** the sentence then decide if the sentence is a statement, question, command or exclamation. Periods end statements and commands. Question marks end questions. Exclamation points end sentences which show a lot of feeling or emotion. **Write** *statement, command, question* or *exclamation* after each sentence.

Lesson 11

Page 71: Alphabetize the English vocabulary words. To alphabetize, write all the <u>a</u> words first, then the <u>b</u>, then <u>c</u>, <u>d</u>, <u>e</u>, and so forth. If two words begin with the same letter then look at the next letter and write the word which has the second letter closest to the beginning of the alphabet.

Page 72: Write the vocabulary word that rhymes with the rhyming word and then write your own rhyming word for the vocabulary word. Rhyming words are words that begin differently but end with the same vowel and ending sounds. For example, *red, bed,* and *said* are rhyming words. They do not need to be spelled the same, but they do need to end with the same vowel and ending sounds.

Page 73: Visualizing what you read will help you remember what you have read. **Read** each sentence then draw a picture of what you see in your mind when you read the sentence.

Page 74: Fluency is the ability to read at a fast pace without stopping much to identify words. With good fluency, a person can think about what he/she is reading instead of struggling with sounding out words. **Practice** reading the story below until you have good fluency. You should be able to read this story in less than a minute. **Read** the words, first going down the columns and then across. Practice reading the words until you can read them smoothly and at a fast pace.

Page 75: Fill in the blanks with the correct words from the story about *Feelings*. **Answer** the following questions in complete sentences. Each sentence must have a subject and a verb. Start each sentence with a capital letter and end it with a punctuation mark.

Page 76: Write the following words in the correct category.

Lesson 12

Page 79: Fill in each blank with a word from the vocabulary page. Use the picture at the end of the sentence to help you.

Page 80: Visualizing what you read will help you remember what you have read. **Read** each sentence then draw a picture of what you see in your mind when you read the sentence.

Page 81: Fluency is the ability to read at a fast pace without stopping much to identify words. With good fluency, a person can think about what he/she is reading instead of struggling with sounding out words. **Practice** reading the story below until you have good fluency. You should be able to read this story in less than a minute. **Read** the words, first going down the columns and then across. Practice reading the words until you can read them smoothly and at a fast pace.

Page 82: Fill in the blanks with the correct words from the story about *Trees*. **Answer** the following questions in complete sentences. Each sentence must have a subject and a verb. Start each sentence with a capital letter and end it with a punctuation mark.

Page 83: Sort the pictures by vowel sounds. Write the name of each picture in the chart under the picture with the same vowel sound.

Lesson 13

Page 86: Fill in each blank with a word from the vocabulary page. Use the picture at the end of the sentence to help you. Read the sentence carefully because you may need to add s or es to the vocabulary word.

Page 87: Visualizing what you read will help you remember what you have read. **Read** each sentence then draw a picture of what you see in your mind when you read the sentence.

Page 88: Fluency is the ability to read at a fast pace without stopping much to identify words. With good fluency, a person can think about what he/she is reading instead of struggling with sounding out words. **Practice** reading the story below until you have good fluency. You should be able to read this story in less than a minute. **Read** the words, first going down the columns and then across. Practice reading the words until you can read them smoothly and at a fast pace.

Page 89: Fill in the blanks with the correct words from the story about *A Kid*. **Answer** the following questions in complete sentences. Each sentence must have a subject and a verb. Start each sentence with a capital letter and end it with a punctuation mark.

Page 90: Fill in each blank with a word from the chart. Use the picture at the end of the sentence or the information in the chart to help you.

Lesson 14

Page 93: Fill in each blank with a word from the vocabulary page. Use the numbers at the end of the sentence to help you.

Page 94: Visualizing what you read will help you remember what you have read. **Read** each sentence then draw a picture of what you see in your mind when you read the sentence.

Page 95: Fluency is the ability to read at a fast pace without stopping much to identify words. With good fluency, a person can think about what he/she is reading instead of struggling with sounding out words. **Practice** reading the story below until you have good fluency. You should be able to read this story in less than a minute. **Read** the words, first going down the columns and then across. Practice reading the words until you can read them smoothly and at a fast pace.

Page 96: Fill in the blanks with the correct words from the story about *Pets*. **Answer** the following questions in complete sentences. Each sentence must have a subject and a verb. Start each sentence with a capital letter and end it with a punctuation mark.

Page 97: Use the words from the chart to fill in the blanks. Read the sentence carefully because you may need to add <u>s</u> or <u>es</u> to the word.

Lesson 15

Page 100: Fill in each blank with a word from the vocabulary page. Use the picture at the end of the sentence to help you. Read the sentence carefully because you may need to add <u>s</u> or <u>es</u> to the vocabulary word.

Page 101: Visualizing what you read will help you remember what you have read. **Read** each sentence then draw a picture of what you see in your mind when you read the sentence.

Page 102: Fluency is the ability to read at a fast pace without stopping much to identify words. With good fluency, a person can think about what he/she is reading instead of struggling with sounding out words. **Practice** reading the story below until you have good fluency. You should be able to read this story in less than a minute. **Read** the words, first going down the columns and then across. Practice reading the words until you can read them smoothly and at a fast pace.

Page 103: Fill in the blanks with the correct words from the story about *Cash*. **Answer** the following questions in complete sentences. Each sentence must have a subject and a verb. Start each sentence with a capital letter and end it with a punctuation mark.

Page 104: Complete each sentence. The verb or subject part of the sentence is missing. After each sentence write **S** if the subject was missing or **V** if the verb was missing.

Example: _____ run in the park.

<u>The kids</u> run in the park.   <u>S</u>

Lesson 16

Page 107: Fill in each blank with a word from the vocabulary page. Use the picture at the end of the sentence to help you. Read the sentence carefully because you may need to add s or es to the vocabulary word.

Page 108: Visualizing what you read will help you remember what you have read. **Read** each sentence then draw a picture of what you see in your mind when you read the sentence.

Page 109: Fluency is the ability to read at a fast pace without stopping much to identify words. With good fluency, a person can think about what he/she is reading instead of struggling with sounding out words. **Practice** reading the story below until you have good fluency. You should be able to read this story in less than a minute. **Read** the words, first going down the columns and then across. Practice reading the words until you can read them smoothly and at a fast pace.

Page 110: Fill in the blanks with the correct words from the story about *Seeds*. **Answer** the following questions in complete sentences. Each sentence must have a subject and a verb. Start each sentence with a capital letter and end it with a punctuation mark.

Page 111: Sort the pictures by vowel sounds. In the chart, write the name for each picture under the picture with the same vowel sound.

Lesson 17

Page 113: Alphabetize the English vocabulary words. To alphabetize, write all the a words first, then the b, then c, d, e, and so forth. If two words begin with the same letter then look at the next letter and write the word which has the second letter closest to the beginning of the alphabet.

Page 114: Fill in each blank with a word from the vocabulary page. Use the picture at the end of the sentence to help you. Read the sentence carefully because you may need to add s or es to the vocabulary word.

Page 115: Visualizing what you read will help you remember what you have read. **Read** each sentence then draw a picture of what you see in your mind when you read the sentence.

Page 116: Fluency is the ability to read at a fast pace without stopping much to identify words. With good fluency, a person can think about what he/she is reading instead of struggling with sounding out words. **Practice** reading the story below until you have good fluency. You should be able to read this story in less than a minute. **Read** the words, first going down the columns and then across. Practice reading the words until you can read them smoothly and at a fast pace.

Page 117: Fill in the blanks with the correct words from the story about *Fun*. **Answer** the following questions in complete sentences. Each sentence must have a subject and a verb. Start each sentence with a capital letter and end it with a punctuation mark.

Page 118: Write the correct action word under each picture.

Lesson 18

Page 120: Alphabetize the English vocabulary words. To alphabetize, write all the <u>a</u> words first, then the <u>b</u>, then <u>c</u>, <u>d</u>, <u>e</u>, and so forth. If two words begin with the same letter then look at the next letter and write the word which has the second letter closest to the beginning of the alphabet.

Page 121: Fill in each blank with a word from the vocabulary page. Use the picture at the end of the sentence to help you. Read the sentence carefully because you may need to add <u>s</u> or <u>es</u> to the vocabulary word.

Page 122: Visualizing what you read will help you remember what you have read. **Read** each sentence then draw a picture of what you see in your mind when you read the sentence.

Page 123: Fluency is the ability to read at a fast pace without stopping much to identify words. With good fluency, a person can think about what he/she is reading instead of struggling with sounding out words. **Practice** reading the story below until you have good fluency. You should be able to read this story in less than a minute. **Read** the words, first going down the columns and then across. Practice reading the words until you can read them smoothly and at a fast pace.

Page 124: Fill in the blanks with the correct words from the story about *A Dock*. **Answer** the following questions in complete sentences. Each sentence must have a subject and a verb. Start each sentence with a capital letter and end it with a punctuation mark.

Page 125: Write the correct action word under each picture.

Lesson 19

Page 128: Fill in each blank with a word from the vocabulary page. Use the picture at the end of the sentence to help you. Read the sentence carefully because you may need to add <u>s</u> or <u>es</u> to the vocabulary word.

Page 129: Visualizing what you read will help you remember what you have read. **Read** each sentence then draw a picture of what you see in your mind when you read the sentence.

Page 130: Fluency is the ability to read at a fast pace without stopping much to identify words. With good fluency, a person can think about what he/she is reading instead of struggling with sounding out words. **Practice** reading the story below until you have good fluency. You should be able to read this story in less than a minute. **Read** the words, first going down the columns and then across. Practice reading the words until you can read them smoothly and at a fast pace.

Page 131: Fill in the blanks with the correct words from the story about *Foxes*. **Answer** the following questions in complete sentences. Each sentence must have a subject and a verb. Start each sentence with a capital letter and end it with a punctuation

Page 132: Fill in the chart with the animal's name. Then place an **X** in each column that applies to that animal.

150

Lesson 20

Page 134: Alphabetize the English vocabulary words. To alphabetize, write all the <u>a</u> words first, then the <u>b</u>, then <u>c</u>, <u>d</u>, <u>e</u>, and so forth. If two words begin with the same letter then look at the next letter and write the word which has the second letter closest to the beginning of the alphabet.

Page 135: Fill in each blank with a word from the vocabulary page. Use the picture at the end of the sentence to help you. Read the sentence carefully because you may need to add <u>s</u> or <u>es</u> to the vocabulary word.

Page 136: Visualizing what you read will help you remember what you have read. **Read** each sentence then draw a picture of what you see in your mind when you read the sentence.

Page 137: Fluency is the ability to read at a fast pace without stopping much to identify words. With good fluency, a person can think about what he/she is reading instead of struggling with sounding out words. **Practice** reading the story below until you have good fluency. You should be able to read this story in less than a minute. **Read** the words, first going down the columns and then across. Practice reading the words until you can read them smoothly and at a fast pace.

Page 138: Fill in the blanks with the correct words from the story about *Sounds*. **Answer** the following questions in complete sentences. Each sentence must have a subject and a verb. Start each sentence with a capital letter and end it with a punctuation mark.

Page 139: Write the correct sound under each picture.

Índice

Alfabético, en orden, 6, 29, 41, 50, 71, 113, 120, 134
Anagramas de oraciones, 55
Comprensión, 5, 12, 19, 26, 33, 40, 47, 54, 61, 68, 75, 82, 89, 96, 103, 110, 117, 124, 131, 138
Familias de palabras, 13
Fluidez, 4, 11, 18, 25, 32, 39, 46, 53, 60, 67, 74, 81, 88, 95, 102, 109, 116, 123, 130, 137
Las Respuestas, 7, 14, 21, 28, 35, 42, 49, 56, 63, 70, 77, 84, 91, 98, 105, 112, 119, 126, 133, 140
Llene el Espacio, 2, 9, 16, 23, 30, 37, 44, 58, 65, 79, 86, 93, 100, 107, 114, 121, 128, 135
Palabras de acción, 29, 62, 113, 118, 120, 125
Palabras que riman, 34, 51, 72
Partes de oración, 62
Plurales, 78, 97
Sonidos vocales, 20, 48, 83, 111
Tipo de oración, 69
Visualización, 3, 10, 17, 24, 31, 38, 45, 52, 59, 66, 73, 80, 87, 94, 101, 108, 115, 122, 129, 136
Vocabulario, 1, 8, 15, 22, 27, 29, 36, 43, 50, 57, 64, 71, 76, 78, 85, 90, 92, 99, 106, 113, 120, 127, 132, 134, 139

Index

Action Words, 29, 62, 113, 118, 120, 125
Alphabetizing, 6, 29, 41, 50, 71, 113, 120, 134
Answer Keys, 7, 14, 21, 28, 35, 42, 49, 56, 63, 70, 77, 84, 91, 98, 105, 112, 119, 126, 133, 140
Comprehension, 5, 12, 19, 26, 33, 40, 47, 54, 61, 68, 75, 82, 89, 96, 103, 110, 117, 124, 131, 138
Fill in the Blanks, 2, 9, 16, 23, 30, 37, 44, 58, 65, 79, 86, 93, 100, 107, 114, 121, 128, 135
Fluency, 4, 11, 18, 25, 32, 39, 46, 53, 60, 67, 74, 81, 88, 95, 102, 109, 116, 123, 130, 137
Plurals, 78, 97
Rhyming Words, 34, 51, 72
Sentence Anagrams, 55
Sentence Parts, 62
Sentence Type, 69
Visualizing 3, 10, 17, 24, 31, 38, 45, 52, 59, 66, 73, 80, 87, 94, 101, 108, 115, 122, 129, 136
Vocabulary, 1,8, 15, 22, 27, 29, 36, 43, 50, 57, 64, 71, 76, 78, 85, 90, 92, 99, 106, 113, 120, 127, 132, 134, 139
Vowel Sounds, 20, 48, 83, 111
Word Families, 13

Books Available From **FISHER HILL**
For Ages 10–Adult

English Vocabulary for the Spanish Speaker Books 1 and 2 were written to help Spanish speakers improve their English vocabulary. *English Vocabulary for Spanish Speakers Book 1* reinforces the vocabulary presented in *English Reading and Spelling for the Spanish Speaker Book 1*, *English Reading Comprehension for the Spanish Speaker Book 1*, and *English Writing Composition for the Spanish Speaker Book 1*. The book is bilingual. The directions are in Spanish with English translations. Spanish speakers increasing their English vocabulary will improve their English reading and listening comprehension and also strengthen their English writing and speaking skills. Good vocabulary skills help people visualize. Visualization helps people remember what is read or heard. Each book is $15.95 and 87 pages. Book size is 8.5 x 11". Book 1 ISBN 978-1-878253-79-8; Book 2 ISBN 978-1-878253-80-4

English Writing Composition for the Spanish Speaker Books 1, 2, 3, 4, 5, and 6 help Spanish speakers improve their English writing skills. Books 1 and 2 begin by teaching basic sentence structure, progress to longer and more detailed sentences, and end with students writing informative paragraphs. This series is good to use with the *English Reading and Spelling for the Spanish Speaker* and *English Reading Comprehension for the Spanish Speaker* series. Price is $15.95 for each book, size is 8.5 x 11" and each book is approximately 152 pages. Book 1 ISBN 978-1-878253-51-4, Book 2 ISBN 978-1-878253-54-5, Book 3 ISBN 978-1-878253-64-4, Book 4 ISBN 978-1-878253-65-1, Book 5 ISBN 978-1-878253-76-7, Book 6 ISBN 978-1-878253-77-4.

English Reading Comprehension for the Spanish Speaker Books 1, 2, 3, 4, 5, and 6 contain twenty lessons to help Spanish-speaking students improve their English reading comprehension skills. Lessons include practice with vocabulary, visualization, fluency, phonology, and comprehension. Each lesson has an answer key. These are excellent books to use after completing *English Reading and Spelling for the Spanish Speaker Books 1, 2, 3, 4, 5,* and 6. Price is $15.95, size is 8.5 x11" and each book is approximately 156 pages. Book 1 ISBN 978-1-878253-37-8, Book 2 ISBN 978-1-878253-73-6, Book 3 ISBN 978-1-878253-74-3, Book 4 ISBN 978-1-878253-47-7, Book 5 ISBN 978-1-878253-48-4, Book 6 ISBN 978-1-878253-50-7

English Reading and Spelling for the Spanish Speaker Books 1, 2, 3, 4, 5, and 6 contain twenty lessons to help Spanish-speaking students learn to read and spell English. The books use a systematic approach in teaching the English speech sounds and other phonological skills. They also present basic sight words that are not phonetic. The word lists are in Spanish and English and all directions are in Spanish with English translations. Each book is $15.95 and approximately 142 pages. Book size is 8.5 x 11". Book 1 ISBN 978-1-878253-66-8, Book 2 ISBN 978-1-878253-67-5, Book 3 ISBN 978-1-878253-68-2, Book 4 ISBN 978-1-878253-29-3, Book 5 ISBN 978-1-878253-30-9, Book 6 ISBN 978-1-878253-35-4

ENGLISH for the SPANISH SPEAKER Books 1, 2, 3, and 4 are English as a Second Language workbooks for ages 10–adult. Each book is divided into eight lessons and is written in Spanish and English. Each lesson includes: vocabulary, a conversation, a story, four activity pages, an answer key, two dictionaries: English-Spanish and Spanish-English, a puzzle section, and an index. Each book is $14.95 and approximately 116 pages. Book size is 8.5 x 11". Book 1 ISBN 978-1-878253-07-1, Book 2 ISBN 978-1-878253-53-8, Book 3 ISBN 978-1-878253-59-0, Book 4 ISBN 978-1-878253-52-1. Book 1 CD ISBN 978-1-878253-55-2, Book 2 CD ISBN 978-1-878253-56-9, Book 3 CD ISBN 978-1-878253-57-6, Book 4 CD ISBN 978-1-878253-58-3

SPANISH made FUN & EASY Books 1 and 2 are workbooks for ages 10–adult. Each book includes stories, games, conversations, activity pages, vocabulary lists, dictionaries, and an index. The books are for beginning Spanish students, people who want to brush up on high school Spanish, or for Spanish speakers who want to learn how to read and write Spanish. Each book is $14.95 and 134 pages. Book size is 8.5 x 11". Book 1 ISBN 978-1-878253-42-2, Book 2 ISBN 978-1-878253-46-0

United STATES of America Stories, Maps, Activities in SPANISH and ENGLISH Books 1, 2, 3, and 4 are easy-to-read books about the United States of America for ages 10–adult. Each state is presented by a story, map, and activities. Each book contains information for 12 to 13 states and has an answer key and index. The states are presented in alphabetical order. Each book is $14.95 and approximately 140 pages. Book size is 8.5 x 11".
Book 1 ISBN 978-1-878253-49-1 Alabama through Idaho
Book 2 ISBN 978-1-878253-11-8 Illinois through Missouri
Book 3 ISBN 978-1-878253-12-5 Montana through Pennsylvania
Book 4 ISBN 978-1-878253-13-2 Rhode Island through Wyoming

HEALTH Stories & Activities in Spanish and English is an English language development book for Spanish-speaking teens and adults. The book contains 19 stories that promote healthy lifestyles and good health. Also included are comprehension, vocabulary, and grammar activities, plus an answer key and index. The book is $15.95 and has 144 pages. Book size is 8.5 x 11". ISBN 978-1-878253-75-0

Fisher Hill
5267 Warner Ave., #166
Huntington Beach, CA 92649-4079
www.Fisher-Hill.com

Purchase Order Number: _____

Bill To:
Name: _____
Address: _____
City: _____ State _____ ZIP _____
Phone: _____

Ship To: (if different than billing address)
Name: _____
Address: _____
City: _____ State _____ ZiP _____
Phone: _____

QUANTITY	ISBN	BOOK TITLE	PRICE	AMOUNT
	51-4	English Writing Composition for the Spanish Speaker Book 1	$15.95	
	54-5	English Writing Composition for the Spanish Speaker Book 2	$15.95	
	64-4	English Writing Composition for the Spanish Speaker Book 3	$15.95	
	65-1	English Writing Composition for the Spanish Speaker Book 4	$15.95	
	76-7	English Writing Composition for the Spanish Speaker Book 5	$15.95	
	74-4	English Writing Composition for the Spanish Speaker Book 6	$15.95	
	37-8	English Reading Comprehension for the Spanish Speaker Book 1	$15.95	
	73-6	English Reading Comprehension for the Spanish Speaker Book 2	$15.95	
	74-3	English Reading Comprehension for the Spanish Speaker Book 3	$15.95	
	47-7	English Reading Comprehension for the Spanish Speaker Book 4	$15.95	
	48-4	English Reading Comprehension for the Spanish Speaker Book 5	$15.95	
	50-7	English Reading Comprehension for the Spanish Speaker Book 6	$15.95	
	66-8	English Reading and Spelling for the Spanish Speaker Book 1	$15.95	
	67-5	English Reading and Spelling for the Spanish Speaker Book 2	$15.95	
	68-2	English Reading and Spelling for the Spanish Speaker Book 3	$15.95	
	29-3	English Reading and Spelling for the Spanish Speaker Book 4	$15.95	
	30-9	English Reading and Spelling for the Spanish Speaker Book 5	$15.95	
	35-4	English Reading and Spelling for the Spanish Speaker Book 6	$15.95	
	07-1	English For The Spanish Speaker Book 1	$14.95	
	55-2	English For The Spanish Speaker Book 1 CD	$12.95	
	60-6	English For The Spanish Speaker Book 1 and CD	$24.95	
	78-1	English For The Spanish Speaker Book 2	$14.95	
	56-9	English For The Spanish Speaker Book 2 CD	$12.95	
	61-3	English For The Spanish Speaker Book 2 and CD	$24.95	
	59-0	English For The Spanish Speaker Book 3	$14.95	
	57-6	English For The Spanish Speaker Book 3 CD	$12.95	
	62-0	English For The Spanish Speaker Book 3 and CD	$24.95	
	52-1	English For The Spanish Speaker Book 4	$14.95	
	58-3	English For The Spanish Speaker Book 4 CD	$12.95	
	63-7	English For The Spanish Speaker Book 4 and CD	$24.95	
	49-1	USA Stories, Maps, Activities in Spanish & English Book 1	$14.95	
	11-8	USA Stories, Maps, Activities in Spanish & English Book 2	$14.95	
	12-5	USA Stories, Maps, Activities in Spanish & English Book 3	$14.95	
	13-2	USA Stories, Maps, Activities in Spanish & English Book 4	$14.95	
	79-8	English Vocabulary for the Spanish Speaker Book 1	$15.95	
	80-4	English Vocabulary for the Spanish Speaker Book 2	$15.95	

Credit Card Information
Card Number: _____
Expiration Date: _____
Name: _____
Address: _____
City: _____ State _____ ZIP _____
Phone: _____

TOTAL _____

Add 7.75% for shipments to California addresses. SALES TAX _____

Add 10% of TOTAL for shipping. (Minimum $6.95) SHIPPING _____

PAYMENT _____

BALANCE DUE _____